D0360493

"A collection of ridiculous and sublime travel experiences."

—*San Francisco Chronicle* Best-Seller List

"These snappy travel stories bursting with candor and crackling humor are sure to leave readers feeling that to not have an adventure to remember is a great loss indeed. *Sand in My Bra* will light a fire under the behinds of, as the dedication states, 'all the women who sit at home or behind their desks bitching that they never get to go anywhere.'"

—*Publishers Weekly*

"Reading about someone else's troubles can be devastatingly funny. And so we have in this volume exotic settings, language-based miscommunication, and not-always-pleasant surprises as things do not go as planned. Despite it all, our band of female travel writers laughs heartily, with pen, paper, and laptop at the quick."

—*Chicago Tribune*

"The writers in *Sand in My Bra* revel in the absurdities of life away from home. F★★k epiphanies; these are the sort of yarns that leave me itching to hit the road."

—*BUST*

"Hip chicks with a flair for storytelling share travel tales in *Sand in My Bra*. From reveling in the 'freedom to be fat' in Tahiti to cycling topless at the Burning Man festival in Nevada, the stories celebrate the unexpected joys of travel from a feminine perspective."

—*Orlando Sentinel*

"Good-natured women find the funny side of mishaps in places as far flung as the red-light district in Bangkok and a 50-pound sack race in small-town Nevada. There are plenty of laughs and—a side benefit—some handy warnings on what not to do when traveling."

—*Portsmith Herald*

"A delightfully entertaining look at atypical travel experiences."

—*South Coast Beacon*

"*Sand in My Bra* supplies laughs as well as a quick fix for the homebound yearning for a quick walk on the wild side."

—*St. Petersburg Times*

TRAVELERS' TALES
HUMOR BOOKS

Sand in My Bra

Whose Panties Are These?

Hyenas Laughed at Me
and Now I Know Why

Not So Funny When It Happened

There's No Toilet Paper on the Road
Less Traveled

The Fire Never Dies

Last Trout in Venice

TRAVELERS' TALES

the thong also rises

further misadventures from
funny women on the road!

TRAVELERS' TALES

the *thong* also rises

further misadventures from
funny women on the road!

Edited by
JENNIFER L. LEO

Series Editors
JAMES O'REILLY AND LARRY HABEGGER

TRAVELERS' TALES
PALO ALTO

Art Direction: Michele Wetherbee/Stefan Gutermuth
Interior design: Kathryn Heflin and Susan Bailey
Cover concept: Peter Ginelli
Cover Photoshop montage: © *Stefan Gutermuth. Jaime McFadden at Montara State*
   Beach, California. (No animals were harmed in the creation of this cover.)
Page layout: Cynthia Lamb using the fonts Bembo and Journal

Distributed by: Publishers Group West, 1700 Fourth Street, Berkeley, California 94710

Library of Congress Cataloging-in-Publication Data

The thong also rises : further misadventures from funny women on the road / edited by Jennifer L. Leo.— 1st ed.
   p. cm.
   Includes index.
   ISBN 1-932361-24-3 (pbk.)
   1. Women travelers—Anecdotes. 2. Voyages and travels—Anecdotes. I. Leo, Jennifer. II. Title.

G465. T66 2005
910.4'082—dc22

2005017952

First Edition
Printed in the United States
10 9 8 7 6 5 4 3 2 1

Dedicated to all the women in the world who overpack
and then make someone else carry it.

Table of Contents

Introduction

I was in the tropical jungle of northern Thailand on a hill tribe trek when I had the opportunity to smoke some opium. And I'm not talking about a handcrafted cigarette in the back of the line while the tour group took a break from the muddy hike…no, this was in a den. An opium den where only the coolest members of the group would be invited in. It was certainly not on the tour description, and that made it all the more appealing.

Visions of a cozy room with long sofas, big velvety red floor pillows, and sheer curtains that gently graced the floorboards came immediately to mind. And the pipes, they would be antiques. I could already feel the grooves of the intricately carved designs with silver and gold detailing. We'd be smoking a family heirloom that literally got passed from generation to generation. Oh yeah, I couldn't wait to get in there. This was a story, this was an adventure, this would be something to tell everybody—but my father—back home. Who cared if I didn't smoke? I'd worry about that technicality later.

The Doctor, a Virginia medical student I'd befriended, motioned for me to follow him. It was time. The anticipation mounted with the same excitement as getting on a fast rollercoaster ride. I was about to set foot in a world of such exotic intoxication that my life and my writing would be forever changed. My hand was already squeezing the cash in my pocket in hopes it would be enough for just one try. We walked up to the straw hut and followed the Thai guide inside. I saw that it was just one room. In the back corner of the hut two Thai men were lying across from each other on thin mats that one might roll up and take to the beach. In front of the smoker's head was a contraption that didn't look anything like a family heirloom or ancient Thai artifact. It was a cut-up Coke can with a candle underneath it. I gasped. This wasn't an opium den, this was a crack house!

See, that's the thing about us eager travelers. The mere whisper of a far-off destination seeps into our heads and swirls around like a cotton candy machine until we have a romantic notion of a trip all big and puffy and sweet. As we book our ticket and pack our bags, we're smiling and humming and most likely flapping our lips about how this is going to be the best trip ever. We've saved our money, we've done all our research, *this* trip is just what we need.

And sometimes it is. Sometimes our dreams come true. Other times, our fantasies turn into miserable itchy unwanted events that are so far removed from a brag-worthy story we feel like we can't come home until we turn it around. Well, we can. Why? Because here at Travelers' Tales we've taken these uncomfortable trips and given them a home. *Sand in My Bra* and *Whose Panties Are These?*—the two previous women's travel humor books in our series— delivered the kinds of stories you were glad didn't happen to you. You laughed, you cried, and you told me that surely there were more types of undies than just our tops and bottoms. Yes, ladies, there are.

At your request, we present *The Thong Also Rises*. The laughs within range from short snickers to laugh-out-loud gut-busters from women who didn't quite get the travel experience they bargained for. Feel free to scream "Eeeewwww!" when Julie Eisenberg gets splashed with urine in a tight cruise ship bathroom in "Princess and the Pee," sympathize with Nicole Dreon in "And Then I was Eight...Again" as she relives being eight, year after year, because her parents are cheapskates, ask Christine Michaud what's best to wear when you're riding a camel in "Travel Light, Ride Hard," navigate the attention of men while traveling solo with Elizabeth Fonseca in "Ravioli Man," and giggle like school girls with Ayun Halliday and her mom as they endure the sounds of Parisian romance in a hotel with thin walls in "Paris, the Third Time Around."

While you're reading these Ms.-Adventures, it is perfectly O.K. to call your friend and tell her you just read something worse than her last disaster. Suggest our series to your book group when you have a busy month and need a break from a heady novel. And especially give our books to someone you know who's hitting the road for the first time. She needs to know that a perfect trip doesn't always make for the best storytelling. In fact, just the opposite. The most important thing is to have fun while enduring the fruits of your folly. And if for any reason you can't laugh in the middle of your misadventure, you'll find that it always becomes funnier as soon as you're back home. For these women whose stories you're about to read, it definitely took a wee bit longer....

—JENNIFER L. LEO

ELLEN SUSSMAN

✦

Naked Nightmare

It's all in your mind. Well, maybe.

MY HUSBAND AND I HAD NEVER BEEN TO A NUDE beach before. Someone at our hotel raved about this place: a white sand beach you could walk along for hours. Naked.

We had already spent a couple of days in St. Martin, soaking up the sun, checking our tan marks at the end of the day. Now we would work on a full body tan.

We drove to the beach in our rented Jeep, following the directions our hotelmates had given us. We were nervous, giddy. Can you do it? Sure. Maybe. Do you think everyone will be scoping out everyone else? Yikes. What about those dimples on my butt? We arrived in the mid-afternoon, parked our car, walked to the closest beach area. The reports were correct: the place was gorgeous. The people were naked. Not just topless. Naked.

We pretended not to look at anyone. Everyone else also seemed to be pretending not to look at anyone. We found a spot of sand, spread our blanket, plunked ourselves down. We took off our t-shirts, our shorts. We glanced at each other.

We were both still wearing our bathing suits. We looked around. Was everyone watching us? Were we the only newbies? Wait—most of the people were sporting very visible tan lines. Perhaps they had just arrived, too, and were all just as scared. I took off my bikini top and lay down flat on the sand, on my belly.

My husband wiggled out of his trunks. Man, he did it. If he could, I could, and so I scooched out of my bikini bottom.

"Is anyone looking?" I asked.

My husband was still sitting up. Easier for him to hide in that position, I noticed.

He shook his head. "Everyone's staring out to sea," he said.

I eased myself into a sitting position. Sure enough, everyone seemed intent on watching the windsurfers, sailors, kayakers, bodysurfers. Then I figured out why—they were all naked! I couldn't imagine how they could feel so unselfconscious, so free. And then I heard the call. *Beer here!*

A topless waitress approached with a tray of ice-cold brew.

"Two please!" I shouted.

She served us, we paid, I drank. Fast. And then I started to relax. I stopped hiding my body. I started soaking in the sun. Soon enough, I wanted another beer. But the waitress was long gone and hadn't returned.

"There must be more beer where that came from," I said.

"I see something all the way at the end of the beach," my husband told me. "Maybe that's the bar."

"I'm going," I said.

"Where?"

"To the bar."

"How?"

"Naked."

I got up, grabbed some bills which I tucked into my fist, and headed off down the beach. Naked.

At first I was terrified. It is hard to walk and cover yourself at the same time. I walked past people who looked at me. All of me. But then, I discovered, I could look at them. All of them. And soon enough, I was swinging my arms, lengthening my stride, feeling the curl of a smile on my face. I was naked! Walking! With strangers! This must be what Woodstock was like! I'm free!

I walked along the beach, easing into my new sense of self. The exhilaration passed but I kept smiling. The bar was ahead of me, at the far end of the beach. I marched up to it and threw open the door. I stepped inside; the door closed behind me. My eyes adjusted to the dark and I looked around.

Everyone was clothed. Everyone was male. Everyone was watching me.

Haven't you had dreams where you're at your job or school or the grocery store and you suddenly realize you've forgotten to get dressed? You wake up. You're like Dorothy, back in Kansas. That was my first thought. This can't be real. Wake up. But someone called for another shot of whiskey and someone laughed and they all kept watching me.

I had two choices. Walk out. Walk on.

I walked across the room and stepped up to the bar. The bartender nodded at me. "Two beers," I said. "And a couple bags of chips." I was amazed that words came out of my mouth. I couldn't believe they could be heard over the pounding of my heart.

"Here you go, sweetheart," he said with a wink.

The bartender took my money. I took the bottles and the bags, turned and walked to the door. In those last few moments I thought: What if I open the door and there is no

nude beach. I've passed into the twilight zone. I'll never return. But the door opened, I stepped out, and the door
closed behind me. Ahead of me, far ahead of me because I
had walked beyond the boundaries of the nude beach, were
my compatriots of flesh.

I ran, bottles clanging, breath caught in my throat. I ran
all the way back to my husband's side, dropped to the blanket, and began to laugh, wildly, nakedly, free.

Ellen Sussman is the author of the novel, On a Night Like This,
a San Francisco Chronicle Bestseller *which has also been published
in France, Italy, Germany, Holland, Denmark, and Israel. Ellen has
published a dozen short stories in literary and commercial magazines
and won a Writers at Work Fellowship. She has published non-fiction
in* Newsweek *and has an essay in* Kiss Tomorrow Hello: Tales
from the Midlife Underground. *She teaches private writing classes
in the San Francisco Bay Area. Her website is www.ellensussman.com.*

✦ ✦ ✦

An American (Drug-Smuggling) Girl

What's that in your bulging bag, ma'am?

"I'm..." I PROCLAIMED LOUDLY AND PROUDLY TO THE man who had a gun secured at his hip, "an AMERICAN!!!"

My mouth was dry, my hands were shaking, and I was scared out of my mind, especially now that the border agent was glaring at me and obviously pretty pissed.

Still standing in Mexico, wishing desperately that I could just fly the five feet to the United States, I realized that I was probably the shittiest drug smuggler of all time.

I totally sucked, but it wasn't my fault.

Merely two weeks before, I went to Walgreens to pick up a prescription for allergy medication and discovered, much to my horror, that the pharmacist wanted eighty dollars from me, which was sixty dollars more than what I paid the previous month.

Now, you know, if I'm going to spend eighty bucks on drugs, I'd better have to show ID and sign my name for the release of a controlled substance. I'd better be walking away with some Vicodin or her delightful cousin Xanax in my

5

little paper bag, not a month's supply of Allegra, which you can mix with alcohol *and nothing happens.*

In my book, that's called "a one-trick-ponydrug."

"You have to be kidding me," I said as I stared at the white lab coat. "I paid less than that to have my gallbladder removed, I got knocked out for that, I got to keep the bedpan *and* a box of tissues. When did sneezing become so expensive?"

"Since Claritin went over-the-counter, the manufacturer of this drug raised its price, and your insurance company decided to make it a third-tier drug, which means it's 'lifestyle enhancing,' and not a necessity, like Viagra," the pharmacist informed me sympathetically.

"Wow, how appropriate," I replied. "The activity of breathing is now considered less important than giving an eighty-year-old a boner. You know, if Allegra was oil, the marines would have invaded and we'd have bombed the manufacturing plant by now."

So when I went home and told my husband that ounce per ounce, Allegra was worth more than cocaine, we decided to stage a standoff. A Mexican standoff.

After all, isn't that one of the perks of living in Arizona, the land where you can die in fifteen minutes of dehydration during the summer if skin cancer doesn't kill you first? But the trade-off is that cheap tequila and pills that we can actually afford are a mere border hop away. Now, I had heard from about a million different people who had all gone to Mexico and come back with all sorts of things—big, giant bottles of Valium, cigarette carton-size boxes of muscle relaxers, antibiotics, you name it—and it was there for the taking. They came back from a Mexican pharmaceutical shopping spree like they were Liza Minnelli the weekend before she was due to check herself into a joint called "Resurrections."

We'll go to Bisbee for a couple of days, we decided, hang out, then swing by Nogales on the way home, grab some lunch and pick up our stash. It was a plan.

It was a bad plan.

After our trip to Bisbee, we pulled into Nogales, and let's just say for the interest of of those who have not been there, border towns aren't exactly known for their glitz and glamour. Suddenly, I felt like I was on a soundstage and at any minute, a grainy image of Benicio Del Toro in cowboy boots was going to cross the street in front of me and Catherine Zeta-Jones would turn the corner with a big creepy cocaine clown in her hand. And mind you, I was still on the American side of things.

We parked our car on the Arizona side, paid five bucks to an old man who looked like he'd sat in that dusty, dry parking lot for so long he'd simply mummified, since essentially all he could move were his eyes.

Now, getting into Mexico is easy, because Mexico knows you're not going to stay. I mean, who really wants to fill out a change-of-address form sporting a zip code south of the border, unless you've just killed your pregnant wife on Christmas Eve, assaulted your scalp with a box of Freida frosting, grown a jaunty goatee, and lost your chubby-hubby pounds to do your best "No, I'm not the guy who killed his pregnant wife on Christmas Eve, I am Ben Affleck, *hombre!*" act? Who really wants to stay there long enough to see if Mexico has seasons? Vincente Fox isn't putting on airs, he knows the score, he doesn't need to shell out extra pesos for any sort of border patrol. Instead, there's just a turnstile. Getting into the Target by my house is harder once you consider the metal detectors.

We went through the turnstile and we were in.

Within five minutes, I had the goods—enough for almost

a whole year, plus some other bonus things I picked up as long as I was there—swinging from my hands in a plastic bag. I was so happy. I was jubilant. I now had the ability to breathe out of one, possibly both nostrils, and for about the same price that my insurance company wanted to charge me for two month's worth of pills.

"I'm a little hungry, do you want to get something to eat?" my husband said.

I scoffed. "Are you kidding?" I said, taking in my surroundings. "I feel like I'm in a United Way commercial. I just saw a *donkey*. To be frank, I really enjoy my intestines in their present, parasite-free condition. Sure, I'd like to lose some weight, but a tapeworm is the last way I'd like to do it, except becoming a prisoner of war. If you have to boil the water here just to drink it, there's no way I'm touching taco meat."

Ready to go home, we walked to the U.S. border checkpoint, which isn't as loose and loving as Mexico's. At all. It's easier to get backstage at a State of the Union address than it is to get back into your country. My husband and I stood in line with the other people ready to be questioned, scrutinized, and searched, and it was just about our turn when I saw it: a sign in black and white that proclaimed that IT IS THE LAW THAT ALL PHARMACEUTICALS AND MEDICATIONS PURCHASED IN MEXICO AND BROUGHT INTO THE UNITED STATES MUST BE ACCOMPANIED BY A VALID U.S. PRESCRIPTION.

I looked at my husband in a panic. He looked at me, then looked at the plastic bag hanging from my wrist.

I had a prescription. I did. It was just two hundred miles away at Walgreens.

"Back to Mexico!" I hissed quickly. "Back to Mexico! Go back to Mexico!"

We bolted out of line and ran back to the marketplace, where we found a seat on a bench and sat.

"What are you going to do?" my husband said. "Do you think the pharmacy will give you your money back?"

I openly laughed. "Not even with a pretty *por favor*," I replied. "I'm stuck. I'm totally stuck. There's only one thing left to do."

My husband looked at me.

"Smuggle," I said, shrugging. "It really isn't breaking the law. I have a prescription. If this goes to trial, I'm sure Walgreens would bring it down to the courthouse. It's either that or try to find a toy manufacturer to get the Allegra compressed and formed into the shape of a clown doll."

"Oh my God," my husband said, shaking his head in disbelief. "Oh my God. Please tell me you're not going to stick a year's worth of Allegra up your ass."

"I wish I could, but with my luck, they'd probably shoot out as bullets. No, they're going into my other black hole," I said as I opened my purse and started shoveling in my purchases. "I've just spent two hundred dollars on this stuff, there's no way I'm leaving it on the bench and walking away."

Back at the border checkpoint, we bravely took our place in line again, and this time, I noticed the cameras all around and above us, which had, without a doubt—in jerky, fuzzy black-and-white Circle K burglary footage—captured our previous appearance in line as we stood for a while, chatted, made fun of the people in front of us, the plastic bag swinging in my hand, then as we suddenly noticed the horrible, horrible sign, reacted with the appropriate melodrama, ran out of line, and then returned five minutes later with no sign of the plastic bag, save for my bulging and giving open purse, me looking as if I were Winona Ryder on a shopping spree or conducting research for a role.

When it was our turn, the border agent motioned us over to his station.

Deep breath, I told myself as we walked to his counter, be cool. Be cool. Stay calm. Act casual. *Do not* act like a smuggler.

"Citizenship?" asked the border agent, a gruff, surly, stocky, and sweaty man, said.

Be cool, I reminded myself.

I stepped forward, my arm outstretched, my driver's license in hand.

"I'm an American!" I proclaimed excitedly, as if I were auditioning for a public service announcement boycotting any products manufactured by the axis of evil. Or France.

The agent looked at me and glanced at my license. "You with her?" he asked my husband, who nodded. "Citizenship?"

"I, as well, am American, sir," my husband said so subserviently that had I not looked at him out of the corner of my eye, I could have sworn he was standing at a full salute.

"What were you doing in Mexico?" the border agent asked as he looked at us with suspicious, angry eyes.

"We ate lunch, sir," my husband, the fake marine, lied.

"You came all the way down from Phoenix to eat lunch in Nogales?" the agent questioned, raising his perspiration-dotted brow. "I don't believe that."

That was the precise moment that the stuttering began.

"No. Ub—ub—ub—ub," my husband, whose face had now turned the color of a hot tamale, said. "Bisbee! We were in Bisbee for the weekend!"

"Bisbee," I added, nodding vigorously. "Bisbee!"

"Did you buy anything while you were in Mexico?" the border agent asked, his eyes narrowing in on me.

I looked back at him, smiled as best I could as my face

flushed with hot, hot fear, nodding and shaking my head at the same time, giving him more of a convulsion than an answer.

He gave up on me and went to his subordinate little puppet, the fake marine.

"Did you purchase anything while in Mexico?" he asked my husband.

"Wa—was—wa—well, I didn't," my husband, the man I am joined with for life, the man whose underwear I wash, the man who just sold me up the lazy river without so much as a fingernail being tugged upon by a pair of border patrol pliers, answered, and then looked at me from the corner of his eye.

"And what did you buy?" the agent said, putting both hands on the counter and leaning toward me. "Did you buy pharmaceuticals?"

I paused for a moment. "Y-y-yes," I whispered, lowering my eyes as my hands started to shake.

"I know you did," the agent replied, smiling a very fake smile, I might add. "Empty your purse, please."

So I hauled out the booty with my sweaty hands, spread it all out as the agent looked on, shaking his head.

"Is this all for you?" he asked me.

"Yes," I nodded as he pointed to one of the boxes. "That's for my allergies. And that…that, is for my asthma. That one is for my back pain. Those are for—um—for—uh, *lady troubles*, and those are because I get these really bad headaches that start on one side of my head and then work their way over to the other side but then eventually I always just end up throwing up anyway."

When I was done spouting off my medical history, I realized I was an eighty-year-old woman from Palm Beach.

"When I asked you if you bought anything, why did you lie?" the agent asked me harshly, clearly very irritated, and it was at this point that I thought he wasn't a border patrol agent after all, but a sales rep from Merck totally pissed off that I had cut him out of his commission.

But I didn't know what to say, and I was so scared I gave him another convulsion, the only thing I had not purchased medication for.

"When you are asked a question, *especially here,*" he said to me quite sternly, "it's in your best interest to tell me the truth! Do you understand?"

"I do," I answered simply as he glared at me, and I had the feeling that I had just lost two hundred dollars and I was going to be talking to a judge very soon. Apparently, I had also taught everyone in line behind me a valuable lesson as they began taking all of their purchases from the *farmacia* out of their purses and fanny packs.

I was convinced that I was going to jail, and I even toyed with the idea of asking the guard if I could take one of my pills before he arrested me because I had a definite feeling I had a throw-up headache charging my way.

I looked at my husband again, and his face was so flushed he looked like he had just had a chemical peel. He had a little mustache of see-through beads gathered on his upper lip, and he was moments away from watching his wife get cuffed as a drug mule because she was just too damn impatient to wait the week it took for Monistat 7 to really work, across the border.

"What can I say?" I imagined myself addressing a jury of my peers. "I want to breathe, I hate to sneeze, and if any one of you has ever been itchy down there, well, you know you would have done the same thing."

And then, against all odds in favor of a miracle at this particular moment, another guard came over to the station and nodded to the guard that was hating me.

"You wanna go on break now?" he asked my mean guard.

"Yeah," my guard said, wiping his brow with his sleeve, then gave me one last dirty look, and simply walked away.

He walked away. Just left us standing there, with all of my medication, enough drugs on that table to start my own rest home. Then the other guard followed him, leaving us alone at the counter.

And that's when I opened my purse, swiped my drugs into it, and very, very, *very* quickly walked away as fast as I could without generating electricity between my thighs.

The narc that I'm married to followed behind by a couple of steps, and when we finally reached the car and got in, neither of us said a word until we were at least ten miles outside of the Nogales city limits.

"We are assholes," my husband finally said, still visibly shaken. "I can't believe we did that. That was horrible! I never thought we'd get out of there. I'm so glad to be out of there!"

"Yeah," I agreed. "No thanks to you, Donnie Brasco! 'No, no, I didn't buy anything. Nope. Not *me*. Not I.' Stoolie!"

"Stoolie?" my husband shot back. "What about you and your 'I'm an *American*!' act? Are you aware that you said it in a *Texas accent*? 'Ah-meh-rih-cahn!!' Oh! Oh! And 'this is for my LADY TROUBLES!' *Lady troubles?* Where *are you*, Charleston, South Carolina, circa 1940?"

"No, I was in MEXICO, about to go to PRISON!" I shouted.

"But yer ehn Ah-meh-rih-cahn!!" my husband shouted. "Who's on more medication than my grandma!"

"You are a dork," I said matter-of-factly.

"No, you are a dork," he retorted. "And you are never going to Mexico again."

"I already know that," I informed him.

"And we are never telling anyone about this, O.K.? No one. No one needs to know what idiots we are. O.K.?" he said firmly.

"O.K.," I agreed.

"Swear?" he insisted.

"On Ah-meh-rih-cuh!" I swore.

Laurie Notaro is currently unemployed and childless and enjoys spending her days searching for Bigfoot documentaries on the Discovery Channel, delights in a good peach cobbler, and has sadly discovered that compulsively lying on her headgear chart in the seventh grade has come around to bite her in the behind. Despite several escape attempts, she still lives in Phoenix, Arizona, where she is technologically unable to set up the voice mail on her cell phone, which she has never charged anyway. She is the author of I Love Everybody (and Other Atrocious Lies) *from which this story is excerpted.*

✳

On our third morning in Paris, I discovered that I was having "feminine problems." Armed with a phrasebook, I marched down to the pharmacy. Swallowing any remnants of American pride and Catholic shame, I began to tell the sweet, bespectacled granny behind the counter that I had an issue "down there" and would need some type of cream. Words were exchanged but we were not communicating. Then, the untranslatable happened. Without warning, *Grandmère* squatted behind the counter, spread her knees, and made earnest jabbing motions with her index finger between her legs. I was so flabbergasted, all I could say was, "Uhh, *non*." We tried a few other more subtle hand gestures until we finally arrived at the same answer and the right medicine. And while I will now always have fond memories of how helpful and kind the lady at my pharmacy was, I pray to all saints in France that I never have to hold another conversation that involves *Grandmère* jabbing at her hooha.

—Cookie Everman, *"Grandmère"*

TAMARA SHEWARD

* ✳ *

Pills, Thrills, and Green Around the Gills

A renegade Aussie in Laos struggles
with the advice of Helen Keller.

AS THE PLEASURE-PAIN MAXIM WOULD HAVE IT, THINGS
went rapidly downhill on our way back to the Mixai, when
we were nearly run over by a *samlor,* pinched on the bum by
a familiar-looking midget, and driven to fits of apoplexy by
a shady monk who sprang out at us from a gloomy alleyway.
Back in our room, the lightbulb burned out and I wound up
stubbing out a cigarette in El's pot of expensive moisturizer.
And after a restless sleep plagued by ravioli-induced nightmares and mosquitos, I could only hope Lady Kismet would
be a bit kinder in the morning.

But Fate's a bitch. We spent the entire morning battling
it out with everyone we came across. Our waitress at breakfast threw a spoon at me after I asked six times for milk. The
cleaner at the Mixai yelled at us for smoking in our room.
And on our way to register our presences with the
Australian Consulate, two kilometers away, our *songthaew*
driver took us on a forty-five-minute junket before charging us ten bucks for the pleasure.

"I think I've had it with city life," I grouched as we pushed open the doors to the consulate. "Even a little pit like Vientiane is getting too stressful for me."

"We should go up-country," El said. "A city is a city anywhere, but we'd get a real feel for Laos if we headed north."

The doors of the consulate slammed shut behind us and we leaned on the unattended front counter. "I reckon. What about that town we read about, the one with the bouncy-sounding name?" As usual, we had no plans and I had no clue.

"I think it's called Luang Prabang. It sounds utterly brilliant and really gorgeous. Hey, is anyone even in here?"

"On my way!" came an Australian voice from behind a heavy office door. The voice was saddled with a less strident ocker twang than Bruce's had been back in Nong Khai, but I cringed anyway. Back in Australia, where we spend so much of our time poking fun at the flat whines of the Yanks and the bizarre vowels of the Kiwis, it's easy to forget we have an accent at all. But spend some time overseas, preferably somewhere they don't broadcast *Home and Away*, and it hits you like a ton of bricks. We sound like freaks. Even in their rare moments of calm, Australian women sound constantly hysterical, and the men manage to give the impression that their words are suffocating somewhere between the glottis and their last meat pie. All this while hardly moving our lips at all.

The door swung open and a well-dressed woman approached us. Apart from the fact that she wore shoes, she looked like a typical Queenslander: blonde, tanned, and hungover. But despite her bloodshot eyes, the woman was polite and efficient, negating my theory about her Queensland origins.

"G'day girls, I'm sorry to have kept you. My name's Louise. How can I help?"

I stared at a framed copy of the words to "Advance Australia Fair" on the wall while El explained that we wanted to register ourselves. "We were told we had to," she finished.

"Well, you don't have to," Louise said. "But it's a good idea. At least then we have an idea of where Australian citizens are when they're in Laos. That way, if anything happens, it makes it easier to identify you."

I winced. "Isn't that a bit dramatic? I mean, what's the worst that could happen?"

"It's just a precaution," Louise soothed. "If you play it safe, you'll be fine. But if you start wandering off into certain areas, you could find yourselves in big trouble. Laos can still be a very dangerous, unstable country."

"Well," El said, "it's not like we're going to wander into the opium fields and start harvesting, if that's what you mean."

Damn, there went all my plans.

"Of course there's that," Louise said. "But that is a bit dramatic. What I mean is that we have posted a traveler's advisory for Australian citizens on a few areas up north where there's been some trouble. If you steer clear of them, you should be just fine."

"Up north?" El asked with a twinge of anxiety. "We were planning on going to Luang Prabang."

"I'd give that a miss if I were you," Louise said. "The highway is too dangerous."

"Why?"

"This actually hasn't come out in the press yet, but in the last week, there's been missile attacks on tourist buses by Hmong bandits."

"What happened?" we gasped.

"Well, these rebels fire at the buses, y'know, blowing them up, and then come and raid what's left for valuables."

Apart from our lives, El and I didn't have anything of value with us. But how were these gun-crazy hill tribers supposed to know that? Strike bus travel. But we were still desperate to get out of Vientiane and into Luang Prabang.

"How about along the river?" El asked. "Can't you take a boat up there?"

"You can," Louise nodded. "But again, we'd advise against it."

"What now?" I whined.

"For a start, it's the dry season and the river is incredibly shallow. The speedboats that travel up it wind up hitting mudbanks and crashing. There was an accident just a fortnight ago."

"What about a slow boat?"

"I was getting to that. This is very much under wraps still, but there was an Australian citizen shot off the top of one of those slow boats only a few days ago."

Jesus. And there I was thinking the worst thing that could happen in Laos was being forced to drink black coffee.

"That's a disgrace," I said, shaking my head. "But hey, what about a plane?"

El nodded at me and looked at Louise, who in turn was staring at us like we lunatics. "You guys really want to get up there, eh?" she said.

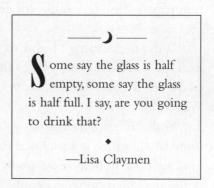

S ome say the glass is half empty, some say the glass is half full. I say, are you going to drink that?

◆

—Lisa Claymen

"Yeah, we really do," I said. Five minutes ago, I hadn't known where I wanted to go. But now, despite, or maybe even because of, the warnings against it, I was chomping at the bit to get to Luang Prabang.

"Well," Louise continued, "let me give you some friendly advice. Don't fly in this country. Don't even go near an airport. Jesus," she shook her head. "It's totally off the record, but listen. Most of the planes in Laos are ancient Russian junk heaps. They're supposedly maintained by the French but I wouldn't go within a bloody mile of them."

We considered our options in silence. We could stay in Vientiane, bored senseless but safe, the able-bodied envy of every cripple in town. Or we could risk life and coveted limb on the airborne equivalent of the Lada for a chance to see the "real" Laos. Ennui versus a fiery death. It was a tough call, but my completely warped sense of logic kicked in and I had my decision. We'd fly to Luang Prabang. At least if we died in a plane crash, we wouldn't be bored.

"I say we do it," I told El, whose smile told me she'd made the same decision. I hoped she'd used a different system of reckoning, though.

"Well, I think you're both nuts," Louise tutted. "But it's your choice. Just fill these in," she handed us our identification papers, "and let's hope we don't need to use them."

"What melodrama," I said to El as we strolled back out into the sunshine. "Old planes fly all the time, no big deal. Look at all those air shows, with planes from like World War II."

"Yeah," El said, hailing a *samlor*. (We figured if they had to pedal, they'd be less inclined to rip us off.) "But have you noticed how nobody ever goes to an air show these days without a video camera? People who don't give a shit about old planes go, just to sell their film to the TV stations in case one of the aircraft explodes mid-air. You see it on the news all the time."

"Oh come on. Is our plane going to loop-dee-loop? Are

we going wing-walking? It's totally different. Besides, don't you want to go?"

"Of course I do. I'm just nervous about getting on some crusty old Russian deathtrap."

"I'm not." And I wasn't either. I'd been to a psychic years before who'd told me I'd live till I was ninety-one. She hadn't mentioned anything about El though.

"Anyway," I said, as we climbed into the waiting *samlor,* "we should remember Helen Keller's famous quote."

"What's that?"

"'Life is a daring adventure or nothing.'"

That's the last time I ever take advice from a deaf, dumb and blind woman—especially one who lived in a time before they invented malfunctioning ex-Soviet bomber planes. It was all well and good for Helen Keller to go around shooting her mouth off about daring adventures, but if she'd seen the rustbucket that we were supposed to spend an hour in at 6,000 feet, I daresay she would have taken dibs on that "or nothing" option.

Cracked, lopsided, and balancing on what appeared to be a pair of deflated tires, Lao Aviation Flight 643 looked more like a warning to pilots about the dangers of flying under the influence than any recognizable means of passage. Slouching beside a sparkling Thai Airways jet, our plane looked like the town drunk hitting up a society lady for some spare change, or at least directions to the nearest flophouse. It was not the most comforting imagery to spring to mind before taking to the skies.

Airport security didn't make us feel much better. After ditching our luggage, we ducked through a metal detector, beeping all the way. The guard took one look at us, scratched his head and moved us along. No emptying of the pockets, no once-over with the electric wand. We could have been weighed down with twenty pounds of gelignite for all that guy knew. Maybe encouraging terrorism was their way of phasing out old planes.

Security on the tarmac wasn't exactly watertight either. Smoking was forbidden in the lounge, so we were sent out onto the runway to puff. Made sense to me. Why choke up a bunch of passengers inside when you can explode a few fuel pumps on the airstrip outside? But it wasn't just smokers wandering around out there. Uniformed men, who I guessed were maintenance crews, lazed in the shadows of baggage trucks, while random people in civvies strolled aimlessly around, examining the underbellies of planes and jumping up to smack the wings. A skinny dog trotted by, sniffed one of the flat tires of Flight 643 and kept going, eventually stopping to relieve itself on a median strip of grass. What a wasted opportunity, I thought. If I'd been allowed to cock my leg in public, I know exactly where I would have been aiming.

"This is just great," I whined, squashing out my butt. "Not only is our plane a total piece of shit, but look at this airport. Anyone could go straight up to our plane, chuck a bomb in the engine and *wham!* A few thousand feet up and we're screwed.

If we can even get off the ground, that is." I lit another fag and exhaled nervously. "Don't they normally have mechanics checking out the plane before boarding? Jesus wept, we would have been better off getting shot off the top of a boat."

El turned to me, her sunburn vanished behind a pall of gray.

"Where's that Valium?" she croaked.

The day after we'd registered with Louise, we'd gone into

town to shake down Trev and buy our tickets to Luang Prabang. By the time we'd gotten to the Lao Aviation office, we were beaming like kids getting ready for a trip to Disneyland. But when they'd charged us double the local's rate for our return tickets, all hell broke loose. El screamed, I glared, but to no avail. If we wanted to go, we had to pay the *farang* fares. So we did. Anything to get up-country, I'd told El afterwards. It'd all be worth it once we were there. But my soothing words hadn't been enough to calm her ire, so we'd marched into a pharmacy and demanded a strip of Valium. It was out of date and crumbling inside it's bubble pack, but it would have to do. I'd stock up on the real stuff later.

"El, are you sure you want some?" Despite my yearning for the pills, I was holding off until I could get some not marked "expiry August 1997." Besides, if the plane did go down, I wanted to be alert enough to get out my camera. El was right. There was big bucks in this plane crash stuff.

She nodded, growing paler by the minute. Judging by my overwhelming sense of nausea, I'd say I wasn't far behind her, but I had my psychic's prediction to fall back on. Granted, this was the same psychic who'd told me I'd have eleven children by the age of twenty-eight, but maybe she was speaking figuratively. If I was going to cark it in a plane crash, I'd know about it.

"Here y'go," I passed El two blue pills and my bottle of tepid water and she gulped them down like a woman possessed.

"Aaaah," she said, as I eyed her cautiously. Well, at least she wasn't dying of chemical poisoning—yet. Things were looking up. If only the plane would stay in that general direction, we'd be fine.

A few moments and a last, rushed cigarette later, our boarding call came through over the scratchy speakers.

"Well," I said, giving El a hand up. "This is it. Let's meet our maker."

I 'll never forget the time I was offered a banger at 30,000 feet. I mistook the intentions of the attractive male flight attendant and replied that I wasn't quite ready yet to join the Mile High Club. His eyes registered horror and all semblance of professionalism vanished in a heartbeat. Cheeks aflame, he then cleared his throat and placed a dish before me containing the weenie that he had actually offered me. I decided to research the inflight Scottish breakfast specials before opening my mouth next time.

◆

—Michele Fontaine,
"On the Road to
Carnal Knowledge"

People always carry on about wanting to die with dignity, but to our fellow passengers on Lao Aviation Flight 643, this was obviously not an issue. With only about fourteen people on board, death would indeed be a private affair, until the networks got hold of the footage, but there was no way one could hope to expire in a courtly or ennobled manner. Resplendent in peeling wallpaper and greasy windows, the cabin was suffocatingly small, which I suppose was appropriate as it matched the seats. Only just big enough to squeeze into, they had neither reclining lever nor room to stretch out, leaving us to sit bolt upright with our legs crossed tightly. We somehow managed to look both stricken with diarrhea and as if we had poles jammed up our arses at the same time. But the Laotians seemed happy enough, relaxing their tiny bodies in the burlap chairs and chatting easily among themselves. If I'd had enough room to comfortably exhale, I would have sighed in relief. Sure, I told myself, these people probably fly all the time. If they're not concerned about the tatty state of the plane, why should I be?

"I'm definitely not scared now, El," I whispered. "The Laotians look cool with this whole plane business, and they should know the score."

El just grunted and I looked over at her. Her eyes were jammed shut and she was biting her lip to a new shade of white. "El, you should open your eyes. It's fine, check out all the happy people." She just shook her head and continued to gnaw her lip. "El, truly, just open your eyes. The first thing you see will be a bunch of chilled out people, same as on any normal flight. It's a good omen, I swear."

With her eyes still clamped, she stood up to stretch and then carefully lifted her lids, staring towards the front of the plane.

"Jesus!" she yelped, slapping her hands over her eyes and collapsing awkwardly back into her seat. "Thanks for the omen," she barked. "Great portent."

"What?"

"Just look up front then give me another Valium. Omen, my arse."

I unbuckled myself and peered up at the front of the plane. Whoops.

Wedged between the cockpit and the front row of seats, an old man lay gasping on a hospital stretcher, with dozens of tubes stuck into every available bit of loose flesh. He looked like a dying fish. He looked like death.

"Oh shit," I said, strapping myself tightly in. "O.K.," I muttered, scavenging through my bag for the pills. "I retract every statement about omens. That guy is *not* an omen."

"Just give me another pill," she said woozily. I handed her

one and she swallowed it dry. "Whoa, yeah," she sighed. "Now that really is better."

As El went back to devouring her lip in silence, I busied myself by plaiting my hair into Princess Leia hoops and looking out the window. I hoped I'd see something more auspicious than the dying old man, but all I could see was that same mangy dog pissing on everything.

"Lady and gentleman, please fasten seatbelt. We will take off soon." I tightened my belt until it nearly cracked my pelvis and grabbed my knees, a mix of fear and strange exhilaration made a rapid departure with the starting of the engines, the violent trembling of the plane paving the way for total domination by fear.

If you're one of those women who gets their jollies by sitting on an operating washing machine, then Lao Aviation has a treat in store for you. You want vibrate, they got it. Thanks to the roaring shudders of the old engines, we vibrated so wildly that I could feel my nostril hairs curling as my spine went numb. Sadly, so did everything else. I never was one for cheap thrills anyway.

"Hold on, El," I shouted above the din of the engines. "Here we go!"

She looked at me through the narrow slits her eyes had become. I must have looked like a psychopath with my juddering head, bug eyes, and braids bouncing all over the place, but I suspected anything would look good to El after her last venture into the realm of the open-eyed. Besides, she was finally, blissfully, stoned. "Princess Leia! You look so cute I could punch you." She said with a dopey smile, and promptly passed out.

Hanging on for dear life as we began convulsing down the tarmac, I felt about as cute as Chewbacca, and nearly as eloquent. Between low moanings, I unconsciously dished up a word salad of curses, blasphemies, and vague promises to a long-neglected God that would have thrilled anyone re-searching the phenomenon of speaking in tongues. At least Chewie always kept a firm grip on his vocab.

Then, somewhere between a particularly vulgar string of obscenities and a since-forgotten vow to lead a more chaste life, the plane took off. It panted and heaved like a huge asthmatic bird, but somehow, we actually became airborne. I peered through the grimy window and watched as Watay Airport began to shrink below us.

"El! El! Wake up! We're in the sky!" I shoved her arm but it just fell limply on to her lap. If expired pharmaceuticals could knock out a panicking person sitting in the world's most uncomfortable chair, I might have to rethink my pol-icy on superannuated medication. After all, 1997 wasn't *that* long ago.

But I decided to stay awake. It was a lucky thing I did. Otherwise, I never would have seen the cabin fill up with smoke ten minutes out of Vientiane. Or felt the grating of the plane's wheels as they came down mid-flight. Or watched the dying old man get beaned by falling hand luggage as we banged down in Luang Prabang. No, if I'd taken Valium that day, I wouldn't ever have become the neurotic freak that I am today. And what a shame *that* would have been.

Tamara Sheward lives in Queensland, Australia. In addition to being a traveler and journalist, she has tried stints at being a toy spider sales-man, Guinness packer, slum lord's subordinate, Rugby World Cup streaker, and smut peddler. She is the author of Bad Karma: Confessions of a Reckless Traveller in South-East Asia, *from which this was excerpted.*

⋆ ✳ ⋆

Cherub

Who was that dastardly criminal?

AFTER MY MOTHER'S MEMORIAL MASS, A YOUNG FRIEND confided that my mother had taught her an important life lesson: never serve cantaloupe on an orange-colored plate. I could just hear my mother: "Oh! Not *that* color, dear," my mother would have told her, deftly switching the cantaloupe slices onto Mexican blue glass. "My first thought," said my friend, "was who cares what color the plate is? But later I saw. Your mother taught me that beauty counts. She taught me that it matters how things look."

It mattered to my mother how things looked one drizzly morning on the island of Capri after early Mass. My eighty-six-year-old father had died suddenly in Italy, and my mother, as a distraction from grief, had taken two of my cousins and me on a trip she had originally planned to take with him. My grief was still dormant. The four of us—three giddy girls and my widowed mother—boarded the ferry from the sleazy, criminal docks of Naples and got off on the magical island of Capri, where my mother would commit her own crime. Capri is famous for being one of the most beautiful islands in the world. Travel guidebooks tell me I should remember steep stone streets, whitewashed walls cascading with roses, crimson bougainvillea, yellow broom, and from every viewpoint, the luminous blue sea lying steeply below. An enchanted island! Instead I remember only three brief unenchanted scenes, each I fervently resented then, each my cousins and I love to remember now, thirty years later.

It was early morning. I was trying to keep sleeping, but my mother was violently shaking my foot. She had turned on all the lights in our low-ceilinged hotel room and was dripping water off her raincoat onto my bedclothes.

"Gina! You've got to get up and help me right now. I've done something terrible."

I sat up fast. This pale woman frantically flinging raindrops, her gray hair wild, was so unlike my cheerful and practical British mother—whom lightning, poisonous snakes, and even war had never been able to rattle—that I was alarmed.

"I've done something awful," my mother said, sitting down hard on my feet. "I've stolen something." My heart flopped into my throat—had my father's death unhinged her? She seemed frantic with distress and my mind filled with preposterous thoughts: Had she stolen jewelry? A gun? Had she *shot* somebody?

I scooched to the foot of the bed. Julie and Tessa and I watched as with shaking hands she opened her straw bag and removed an object hidden under her scarf. "Oh, dear," she said, unveiling the object of her crime. And here it was: a five-inch-high pink plastic dashboard mascot of a roguish little boy. He was holding his outsized dick in his hand and pissing into a little toilet. By means of the handle on the toilet, the penis of this fiendish boy could be ratchetted up or down. Coming out of early morning Mass, glowing with the beauty of the sacrament and the fresh Capri dawn, my mother had stepped into a shop to buy postcards. This hideous toy, grinning at her from the cash register, had struck her like a blow. She had told the shopkeeper it was a shame to have such a thing in such a beautiful setting. She had offered to buy it from him. No, he had said, shrugging, it was a present from a friend. And then he had turned his back. It had taken her only a moment to commit her crime, to swish the ugly thing into her big straw bag and hurry out into the wet street.

I was outraged and pushed her off my feet. For this she got me up? But my mother was in a frenzy of anxiety.

"What if he saw me?" she says. "What if he told the police? What if it gets into the papers?" She imagined the headlines for us, something like this: PROFESSOR'S WIDOW STEALS OBSCENE TOY. "Gina," she said, "you've got to go right now and explain to that man. Apologize for me."

Now I was scared. Was my mother coming unglued? Why did she have to go and do this crazy thing? And now she wanted me to fix it. But I was proving good at denial these days. "I need more sleep," I told her. "I'll take it back later."

"We're not *taking* it back," she said. "I just want you to explain to the man and apologize for me. Tell him his island of Capri is so beautiful that he shouldn't have such an ugly thing on his cash register. It doesn't belong. Offer to pay for it." She opened her wallet, her British self again, mustering her troop.

"It doesn't *matter* what's on a store's cash register," I argued, exasperated now. "It's his store."

"Yes it does," said my mother firmly. "It's ugly and we're

not giving it back." She wasn't suffering from madness after
all, I realized, just grief and offended aesthetics.

I got resentfully out of the cozy bedclothes. With very bad
grace, I took the envelope of lire my mother handed me.
Perhaps I even looked up *crazy* in the Italian dictionary. Then
I put on my shorts and sweater and stepped out onto the
drizzly street. I was aware that I was being a graceless daughter, that Julie or Tessa, who were devoted to my mother,
would have *embraced* the mission of clearing her name. But I
was the one who spoke a little Italian. I walked across the
cobbles towards the shop, rehearsing my speech, full of dread.
And then an idea occurred to me—a way to postpone the
moment of walking into the shop. A gesture that might almost redeem me in my own eyes. Minutes ticked by as I
ducked in and out of tourist shops, hoping that my cousins
were worrying at my delay and not enjoying breakfast without me. At last I lit on another boy-statue, this one a terra-
cotta cherub, genderless, mostly wings.

Armed with my bland cherub, I crossed the street and
walked fast into the pillaged shop and straight to the counter
before I could lose my courage. But the shopkeeper was talking to a friend, which gave me time to be nervous, time to
look at the cash register, where the nasty boy must have
been, time to wonder—absurdly—how the shopkeeper
could even *keep* shop, as though nothing had happened, with
his interesting mascot missing from right under his eye. Time
to wonder whether he knew already the reason that brought
me here, while he chatted deliberately on and on.

Finally, the friend moved away from the cash register. I
stepped forward, my cherub in hand. I pushed the envelope
of lire across the counter, and then I unwrapped the cherub.
"This is for you, *signor*," I told him. "My mother," I said,
pointing to the empty spot, "has stolen your boy. She is *matta*,

crazy," I told him in broken Italian, dancing my fingers on either side of my face to show him crazy. "My father is dead," I told him.

"*Bene, bene*, it's all right," he told me, mostly bored. But I pressed the modest cherub on him. "*Non, signorina.*" He didn't want it and tried to give it back to me. "Take it!" I said, and fled from the shop. In the drizzly street I cried for a long time, for my father, for my mother, for my unkindness in not recognizing her theft as a symptom of grief. Then I wiped my eyes and went back to the pensione.

On the night we left Capri, my cousins and I leaned over the white ferry railing. The black water was foaming far below us as we ploughed away from the magical island, and we had a job to do. "Here he is!" said Julie. In a moment, she and Tessa were merrily balancing the toy on the railing, pushing the tiny tank handle up and down a last few times. My mother's crime embarrassed me still, and my own unsympathetic heart, but then I was laughing, too, as the three of us, with a giddy hoot, consigned the unzipped boy to the waves.

Gina Briefs-Elgin teaches composition and creative nonfiction at New Mexico Highlands University in Las Vegas, New Mexico. She writes about travel, confectionary, the decorative arts, and the literature of mysticism. Her favorite activities are traveling with her husband and son, riding Amtrak, and fishing trout streams (although it dismays her to catch anything).

NICOLE DREON

* * *

And Then I Was
Eight...Again

Childhood can last forever.

THE IDEA OF BUDGET TRAVEL AS A NOVELTY WOULD
appall my mother. A lifelong penny pincher, coupon clipper,
and notorious tightwad—even Arthur Frommer's prudent
advice pales in comparison to my mother's frugality. Were
she the Queen of Sheba, she would bellow from her
deathbed, "How much for the casket?" before proclaiming
emphatically, "That's ridiculous," and croaking.

Her fiscal woes were only complicated by my father's own
neuroses—a man who would routinely sprint up mountain
peaks just to declare himself the winner; then, unabashedly,
relieve himself in front of the Cleaver's Sunday picnic while
they pondered whom he was racing. As a family we embraced nature with the same fleeting satisfaction one might
allot a McDonald's Happy Meal. Had Henry David Thoreau's
Walden appeared in our car on a family vacation, we'd have
balled up the pages and used them as toilet paper. "Don't
worry," my mom would have assured us, "you've seen the
movie before. It's the sad one with Jane Fonda."

"But Mom," my brother and I would have howled in unison, "the paper hurts when we wipe."

The consequences of such parenting were a seamless blur of childhood vacations spent sling-shotting across the country. The routine was always the same. Right before the park entrance we'd slow to a crawl, Mom would lean over and read the sign through her coke bottle glasses and sigh, "Ages eight and under free." Knowing what came next, I'd cry out immediately, "No, no, no, I've been eight for three years!" It didn't matter. In our family, my brother and I were like ageless movie stars. I once asked my mother what year we visited Yellowstone, and she replied, "When you were eight and your brother was six." Shortly thereafter, I found a photo of our family in front of Old Faithful—my brother had a beard.

One of the summers when I was eight and my brother was six the car we called "Lemon" had the audacity to overheat in Badlands, South Dakota. Besides throwing a crimp into our packed agenda, it left us stranded, like the cliché, on a lone desert highway. When we piled into the front seat of the tow truck, my and Allen's skinny legs dangled limply above the floorboard. Mom squished up against Dad with the window rolled all the way down.

We had an Aunt Sherry who lived outside of Rapid City, and Mom informed us we would be staying with her until Lemon got fixed. Allen begged her to take us to a real hotel like the one in Cincinnati with the vibrating beds. I asked who Aunt Sherry was and why we'd never heard of her. "She's your Uncle Jack's first wife," Mom told us, "they were divorced before you were born." We'd never met Uncle Jack either. I'd only ever heard Mom talk about him in that tone she used with her adult friends. "The last one he married was going to get deported," she'd say. "He was old enough to be her father."

Aunt Sherry came to get us in an old blue pickup. Allen and I rode in the back and ping-ponged around the truck bed every time she pumped the brakes. "You two O.K.?" Mom would holler from inside the cab every now and again. Aunt Sherry wore short cut-off jeans and cowboy boots, and we could see her boobs through her t-shirt. They weren't like the boobs in Dad's nudie magazine, the same magazine I once whipped out in front of our babysitter and she nearly died of a coronary. "What," she gasped, horrified. "What would your father say if he knew you were reading *Playboy* at the dinner table?"

"He lets me read the articles," I lied and then tried not to spill macaroni on the grown-up girl's privates. No, Aunt Sherry had real swingers, more like my mom's, and it made Allen and me giggle.

It felt like forever before we finally pulled into Aunt Sherry's driveway. She hopped out first, and Allen and I staggered to stand up on our sea legs. "Now you kids," Sherry spoke to us slowly, "stay away from Bruno the attack dog and don't go near his duck 'cuz they are friends. And if the geese give you any trouble wave your arms in the air and pretend to be bigger." As soon as I heard the words dog and attack in the same sentence my hands got clammy and my eyes rolled back in my head.

"Oh come on, Colie," my mom tried to coax me out of the truck two hours later, "you can't stay out here all night." I could and I would. I could not fathom being mauled or pecked to death.

"The rattlesnakes will get ya, if ya stay out here at night," a deep voice rumbled that apparently belonged to my Uncle Brooks. Uncle Brooks wore black socks with sandals and his legs were plastered with mosquito bites, but his authority on rattlesnakes had me bee-lining for the house.

"Do I look bigger than the geese?" I screamed mid-sprint, flailing my arms in the air. "Dad, open the door, here I come."

"You look like a big 'tard is what you look like," Dad scolded when I reached him. "Run with your arms down, sissy, it's faster."

"Oh honey," Sherry said soothingly. "The geese are out back for the night."

Two days had passed when Aunt Sherry decided she had had enough of us asking why there were thirteen dressers in one room and none in another, or why we couldn't drink water from the tap, or why Uncle Brooks only wore one sock when he fell asleep in the yard. "We're going to the pool," she announced after breakfast. "Get your little swimmers on, let's go."

"Yippie, yippie," Allen and I jumped up and down. "Let's go, let's go."

For as long as I can remember my dad and brother wore matching Speedos to the pool—a father/son ritual our whole family agrees haunts my brother to this day. Dad would parade around proudly in front of the pool girls when Mom had her glasses off; my brother's little orange trunks fell off without fail on the slide. By the time we reached puberty, we forbade our father to sit with us at the beach. "Don't come near us in that ball buster," we'd warn him.

"All the Canadians wear Speedos," he'd tell us proudly. "Why shouldn't I?"

"Because you're not Canadian, Mr. Banana Hammock, now beat it."

"Would you two be nice to your father," my mother would murmur without looking up from her book and then Dad would sulk and head farther down the beach.

Aunt Sherry knew everyone at the community pool in Rapid City, and she was still gabbing at the concession stand when we stripped off our nylon shorts and scurried for the shallow end. My feet burned on the pavement so I ran faster; Allen clasped the sides of his Speedo and tried to keep up. We didn't get out of the water until Aunt Sherry offered us a popsicle. "I want cherry," I told her, and she started rummaging through her purse.

"This looks red," she announced and surfaced with a dripping piece of wax paper from the depths of her big, black body bag.

On the way home, Mom was worried because Aunt Sherry was talking funny and the brakes in the truck still didn't work. When we pulled into the driveway, Uncle Brooks was sprawled on the lawn like a rotting carcass. His comb-over was wafting in the breeze, and Bruno's duck was pecking at his head. When he suddenly sat up and started sputtering, "What the hell...what the hell are you people doing up so early?" we all jumped back in our seats.

Sherry staggered out from behind the wheel and hollered at him, "Brooks you dumb shit, it's four in the afternoon."

"Well goddamn," Brooks coughed dumbfounded. "Well goddamn if it is."

Later that night, Sherry didn't take the chicken out of the freezer in time to defrost for dinner, so we had hot dogs outside on the picnic bench. Brooks stood on the lawn chair and vacuumed bugs off the lantern, while we shouted at each other like old people.

By morning Dad was on the phone with Lemon's mechanic, and he had that serious look on his face. Mom stood behind him whispering, "How much? How much?" and he motioned her away. Allen and I had a new game where we took turns jumping on the couch to make dust clouds. "Aunt Sherry," Allen blabbed during bounces, "at night when we're camping, Mom pees in a bucket in the camper." I started howling until Mom slapped my leg.

We left Aunt Sherry's at dusk because Dad didn't want to drive Lemon during the day when it was hot out. We spent the next four weeks touring the country in the dark like a band of little refugees. First, though, we headed to that place where the faces were carved into the mountain. "Whose faces are they, Dad?" we asked anxiously.

"A couple of ugly guys with big noses," he told us.

"Do I have to be eight?" I probed.

Mom yawned and answered, "We'll have to wait and see."

Nicole Dreon works for ESPN's X Games in their research department, where she interviews adrenaline junkies on a regular basis. She is an East Coast transplant who headed west after college in search of cowboys, but is still single nine years later due to her fear of horses. Nicole recently climbed and worked on a documentary film about the Rwenzoris Mountains of Uganda. The only time she's set foot in an office was to work for Points North Heli-Adventures in Alaska, where she traded a paycheck for heli-time. When she's not on the road, she calls Truckee, California, home.

*

We woke up at daylight a few hours later to the sound of the roosters. I rolled over and noticed a familiar image. Blonde hair, blue eyes, a perfect smile, and an absurdly proportioned figure. Barbie sheets! I LOVED Barbie throughout childhood and may even harbor a secret desire to be Barbie with her great life, car, townhouse, wardrobe, and boyfriend Ken. She can do anything. And here I was in the middle of the jungle in Bolivia sleeping on Barbie sheets. I never had Barbie sheets at home. I was never even allowed to have the Barbie car or townhouse. This was true splendor. When we finally got ourselves out of the Barbie comfort, we went to inquire with the hotel owner about the river boats. The owner sent us down to the river, but mentioned that she didn't think that the boats were running this time of year. We checked out the small town. Small houses built of wood with thatched roofs, animals running around, and beautiful vegetation. Not a tourist in sight. We were lucky there was a hotel there. With Barbie sheets no less.

—Joanna Popper, "The Back of the Bus with Mom"

JENNIFER COX

* ✱ *

Hot Date with a Yogi

She was dripping with sweat but beset
by a wardrobe malfunction.

NATHAN TAUGHT BIKRAM YOGA, THE INDIAN DISCIPLINE
of yoga in a room heated to 100 degrees (the idea being that
it relaxes your muscles, releasing trapped toxins and allowing
you to efficiently sweat them out). I'd been put in touch
with Nathan through my friend Kate at the Australian
Tourist Commission in Sydney.

Our date was tonight, but in his message Nathan suggested I come to his class that afternoon, then we could go
straight on to our date afterward.

Unfortunately, I'd had my phone switched off. Date
Protocol: I felt it was bad form to take a phone call from
your next date while the current one was still in progress—
and now it was already afternoon. I stuck out my arm and
hailed a cab downtown.

I arrived at the Bikram center with five minutes to spare.
As I dashed up the steps, I caught sight of a completely
gorgeous man disappearing into a room, steam already
condensing madly on the windows. He was followed by a

group of star-struck women (and a couple of men). If that was Nathan, I could see why the class was so popular…and why the classroom was hot and steamy. (I'm always happy to embrace my *inner shallow.*)

But I'd been in such a rush I hadn't given any thought to what I was going to wear. The bra I had on was O.K., but no way was anyone going to see me going lotus wearing a thong.

I went careening over to the woman sitting at the reception desk (so far, yoga was proving anything but relaxing) to see if they had a spare pair of shorts I could borrow. No, but "go to Gowers on the corner," she told me shortly, looking with disapproval at her watch. "They're real cheap and you'll pick up some shorts for nothing. Once the class has started, you can't go in, though, so quick go, go," she shooed.

I raced across the street to Gowers, but all I could find cheap was a nasty pair of men's gray Y-fronts. I held the packet at arm's length and examined it speculatively. Nathan was gorgeous and these men's briefs were ugly, ugly, ugly. But I'd never wear them again and they were only nine dollars, so sod it, I was in a hurry. I shoved some cash at the sales clerk and dashed back to the center. In the changing rooms I ripped the knickers out of the package, and, without stopping to inspect them, shoved them on, pulled my top off, grabbed my bags, and bolted for the yoga room.

I got to the doors just as they were locking them. There wasn't time to introduce myself, so I quickly walked into the class, past mats full of limbering ladies to a free spot at the front of the class, and sat down.

Nathan stood before us, lithe and muscled to the point of being edible. As he walked us through the first positions, I attempted to bend my upper body over my extended thighs.

As I strained downward, I caught sight of my pants for the first time. The thick gray flannel was so stiff that the Y flap at the front was poking straight out in a disturbingly suggestive manner. Embarrassed and trying not to draw attention to it, I quickly reached down and pushed the flap back into place.

But it was having none of it and sprang straight out again, veering purposefully like the rudder on a sailboat.

It was horrible. I tried another tack: Leaning into my stretch, I surreptitiously attempted to pin the protruding piece of material flat with my elbow. But it was impossible to concentrate on both this and the yoga, and the front of the pants sprang straight out again, wagging from side to side, like the tail of a dog happy to see you.

The room was as hot as a furnace by now, and soon the pants were thoroughly soaked in my sweat, turning the dark gray flannel an even darker gray—apart from the flap at the front, which, since it wasn't in contact with my body, remained free from sweat and light gray, sticking out in lewd shamelessness.

After what seemed like an eternity, the class ended. And—all credit to me—I was brave enough to stay behind and introduce myself to Nathan. But as I hadn't thought to bring a towel for the shower or any clean clothes, our date ended up too *yin and yang* for comfort: He was serene and self-aware, I was sweaty and self-conscious. I stayed for one drink, then went back to the hotel, lay on the bed, and watched *When Harry Met Sally* on TV, using biscotti as spoons to eat a tub of ice cream.

Jennifer Cox spent many years juggling two jobs, one as a BBC travel journalist and the other as head of public relations for Lonely Planet, before deciding enough was enough and traveled the world in search of love instead. A correspondent for BBC's Holiday, co-host of BBC1's "Perfect Holiday," and a weekly commentator for Sky News, she has written for publications including The London Times, Marie Claire, Elle, Esquire, *and* Cosmopolitan. *This story was excerpted from* Around the World in 80 Dates. *Jennifer now happily juggles her old London life with her lovely new one in Seattle.*

✳

Because dinner didn't take as much time as we'd planned, we now had an hour to kill before the show. I'd made the mistake of buying new shoes for the trip and my feet were already hurting. Not only were the shoes brand new, they were also a size and a half too small with four-inch heels. The saleslady at BCBG, Katarina, had talked me into buying them, "They are a very sexy shoe on you and because of the length of the pant, you need the high heel." And I needed the pants because, according to Katarina, "They make your backside look very good!" (I thought it only a matter of time before Katarina and I began dating.) Of course I couldn't tell Hank any of this. His response would simply have been, "Well then, take them off." As if I could do that after spending $200 on the outfit. Ha! I wished.

"Hey, wanna go back to the room for a bit? I mean, since we have an hour until the show and everything," I asked Hank, grabbing a hold of his shoulder and trying not to wobble.

"Sure," Hank said, probably hoping this was code for "Hey, wanna go back to the room and have sex before the show?" When it was in fact code for "Hey, my feet are killing me. I need to get these shoes off."

—Elizabeth Ellen, "Pain and Fumbling in Las Vegas"

* * *

Riding the Semi-Deluxe

*Didn't your mother tell you to go
at the very first opportunity?*

IT WAS A WARM, BRIGHT MID-MORNING AND I WAS bumping down the road on a semi-deluxe bus. My fellow passengers nodded at me in a friendly manner, I had a mango Frooti drink and a roll of chocolate-chip biscuits to snack on, and the scenery of goats and huts and sari-clad women was picturesque. Exactly the sort of bus experience I had imagined when I planned my trip to India. The only problem was I wasn't entirely sure where I would end up. And I had to pee.

I was hoping to get to Gokarna, a beach town in South India which, according to an Australian girl I'd met in Delhi, was supposed to be a tranquil, relaxing place, a Goa without the rave kids. As a solo female traveler who had been overwhelmed by crowded, grimy Delhi and who had a low tolerance for trance and techno, I thought it sounded great.

The trip had seemed simple enough when I started out in Hampi. I successfully took the 7 A.M. bus to Hospet, where I was supposed to get on the 9 A.M. bus to Gokarna.

But in Hospet the plan crumbled. After an hour and a half of confusion and contradictory announcements, it was official: the Gokarna bus was cancelled.

A crowd gathered to discuss my options. Some thought I should take a bus to Sirsi and then transfer, and others argued for taking a bus to Kumta to transfer. A minority was against both of these plans. I was worried about getting stuck in some tiny town with no hotels and no ongoing buses, but when I asked about this either nobody understood the question, or I didn't understand the answer. Anyway, my input wasn't under consideration in the matter. What did a foreign tourist know about anything, even if she did look almost Indian? When the shouting died down, the pro-Kumtas and the fringe parties had been overruled. I was put on a bus and told to transfer at Sirsi. "Don't worry," said the station manager, "The driver will get you to Gokarna." So I was on a bus, at least, and I had a flimsy promise to hold onto, and hopefully there would be a bathroom stop along the way.

The first stop was a lonely roadside restaurant full of scowling men. Around back, in the middle of a field, a decidedly non-picturesque concrete wall shielded three doorless toilet stalls from view of the restaurant. I stepped behind the wall.

Shit.

There was shit everywhere. In the squat toilets, on the footrests, around the toilets, on the concrete floor between the wall and the stalls. Shit, in globs and heaps and puddles and mounds, every color of the shit rainbow. I stared for a while, thinking longingly of the restroom at Hospet, where an old woman was employed to pour a can of water over the concrete toilets after every use. "I'll just wait for the next stop," I thought.

The next stop was an hour later at a similarly lonely location. The toilets there were free of fecal matter, but had instead been taken over by spiders. Webs festooned the rafters,
stretched across the stalls, blocked the doorways, and
crowded the corners, each presided over by a plump, black,
jellybean-sized spider. Unlike their apathetic daddy-long-
legs cousins who hang motionless for weeks at a time, these
spiders were busy. Industrious. Moving. Even someone without a spider-phobia as strong as mine would have been
freaked out. I kicked myself for being too picky to use the
last toilet. I mean, what's a little shit?

If it had been dark, or if I had been wearing a long skirt,
or if I had a travel buddy, or if I were a man, I would have
just gone in the field behind the bathrooms, but none of
those things was the case, so I got back on the bus. No matter what confronted me, I promised myself, I would use the
bathroom at the next stop.

Another hour passed jouncing over potholes and wishing
I hadn't had that mango Frooti. Tree branches scraped past
the open windows and sifted a fine dust onto me as I wiggled and worried. What would be worse, I wondered, being
stranded overnight or wetting myself? I wished there was a
toilet on the bus. Semi-deluxe, I decided, must be a eu-
phemism for not deluxe at all.

At last we drove into an actual town, with a real bus station like the one at Hospet. I had high hopes for this station's
facilities, hopes that rose even higher when I saw that said
facilities were actually indoors and that people were actually
going in and out of them. In fact, the area positively boiled
with activity. Vendors hawked bananas and nuts and newspaper cones of puffed rice, bottles of Thums Up and Limca,
strings of the tiny white flowers that South Indian women

affix to their glossy dark braids. One problem solved, I thought as I galloped off the bus and across the lot.

Inside the women's end I found three stalls with doors on the far side of the room and three doorless squat toilets on the near side, separated from each other by low walls. A baby girl squatted in the toilet closest to the door, displaying remarkable balance for such a tiny thing. Two older girls, maybe eight and ten, dark-eyed and pretty, exchanged smiles with me. I headed to the stalls with doors first, but found them inhabited by more of those spiders. The middle toilet even had some shit floating in it for good measure. It didn't occur to this privacy-loving American girl to use one of the open toilets, so I was reduced to an uncertain shuffling.

As I stood there, a woman in a gold-shot sari entered the restroom. Regally, elegantly, she squatted over the drain in the middle of the floor and urinated into it, her sari providing a remarkable amount of privacy for

—— ☽ ——

The first time I used a washroom in Japan, I pulled the toilet paper and nearly fell over backwards into the toilet. Music was definitely not what I was expecting, much less Beethoven. That's right, bars of "*Für Elise*" chimed out happily as I steadied myself in shock. I really wanted to ask someone about it, but how do you go about doing that without being rude? Everyone knows about the polite factor in Japan, and besides to them, music in the toilet is normal. So I saved the story for my friends back home, who found it quite amusing.

◆

—Catherine Tully,
"Painfully Obvious"

someone peeing in the middle of the room. She fixed a gaze of disdain on a point in the middle of the wall like someone undergoing a disgusting but necessary medical examination. Finished, she stalked back out the door without acknowledging anyone's presence. Even the jewel in her nose glittered a little sneer. I should do that too, I thought, impressed. But how could I? Seeing my hesitation, the older girl poured some water over the muddy footrests of one of the open toilets near the door and indicated that I should use it.

Just then a big gray pig walked in the door. I don't know how big pigs are supposed to get so I can't say for sure where this one stood in the spectrum, but if it had been a dog it would have been a pretty huge dog. The pig made straight for the baby and started snuffling around her, eliciting a shriek of terror and nearly knocking her into the toilet before one of the girls scooped her to safety. Apparently disappointed, the pig veered off to the stalls on the other side of the room and poked its head into the first stall, and then the second. Now, I had heard rumors about certain porcine dining proclivities, but I was still shocked by what I saw next. "What is it doing…it's not going to eat the…oh yuck…" I watched for a while in disgusted fascination as the pig gobbled down the contents of the toilet.

Oh well. I seemed to be the only one who found the pig's presence or behavior surprising and I still had to go. The girls looked at me expectantly. I waited for them to discreetly busy themselves elsewhere, but finally I realized they were planning to watch the whole process. I was not too keen on this idea, but I had no choice. I could not possibly hold it in for another hour. It's a natural function, I told myself. Everyone does it. Besides, they're little girls, not spiders.

Resigned, I stepped onto the newly rinsed porcelain footrests and pulled down my pants.

The pants. Bought in Hampi solely because my long skirts hindered a bicycle tour of the ruins, they were the most hideous article of clothing I could imagine—a baggy, elastic-waisted, narrow-ankled, multi-colored cotton nightmare that made me feel like a giant hackeysack. The shop owner had seemed to think I would be delighted to purchase a pair of "Indian" pants, but anyone with the gift of sight could see that no Indian woman, or even an Indian man, ever wore such a garment. Their saving grace was that they were comfortable, and that's why I had worn them on the bus trip. And now the hideousness of the pants would be highlighted as I pulled them down in front of two eagle-eyed little girls who were about to watch me go to the bathroom all wrong.

There is a correct way to squat, with your butt very close to the ground, your hamstrings pressed against your calves and your feet flat. Once you master this position, it's quite comfortable, but I could only achieve it sporadically. Weighing the embarrassment quotient of peeing incorrectly against peeing correctly but possibly falling into the toilet, I chose to pee wrong and stay clean. I squatted awkwardly, with my feet bent uncomfortably and my behind way too far up in the air. Under the rapt attention of my audience, curious as a couple of scientist kittens, I needed to find something else to focus my attention on. The most interesting thing in the room had to be the big, gray, shit-eating pig, so that's what I looked at.

Then two things happened simultaneously. One was that the pig finished her meal and started trotting towards me. Pigs are smart and this one obviously knew the area well. I didn't need Pavlov to tell me what she was hoping for.

The other thing was that a bus began honking its horn. I had no way of knowing if it was my bus or not, but it could have been. It must have been. Of course it was. The pig would knock me into the toilet and my bus would leave and I'd be stranded in the middle of India wearing hideous pee-soaked clown pants while the town's little girls gathered around to stare at me.

The pig came at me, her snout decorated with what looked like beads of chocolate milk. I was stuck; I couldn't escape. I peed frantically, trying to finish so I could flee, but I'd been saving it up for a long time and anyway, you can only pee so fast.

But then the girl who had cleaned off the toilet for me came to my rescue, shaking her water bottle at the pig. Surprisingly, and a bit anticlimactically, her tactic worked; the giant pig backed off under the threat of a small, empty, plastic bottle and trotted out the door. That was good. Then the bus stopped honking. That was not so good, at least, not if it was my bus and if the silence meant it had given up on me.

Finally I was finished. Pulling my clothes together, I raced for the exit. The older girl headed me off at the door and politely asked for two rupees. A small price to pay. I gave a rupee to each of the girls. Then I was outside, rounding the corner, searching out the spot where my bus had parked.

It was gone. Gone, with my non-ugly clothes and my journal and my camera and my chocolate-chip biscuits from Hospet and my Walkman and my mix tapes. I was stranded. I cursed the bicycle trip that had forced me to buy those wretched pants, now the only clothes I owned.

Then I saw my bus. Halfway out of the lot, engine running, windows bristling with a dozen frantically beckoning arms. I took a deep breath of relief and started to run for it, but a little boy blocked my way, running backwards and chirping, "Hello, one rupee! Hello, one rupee!" over and over again like a mantra. He giggled and bounced like it was all a big game. But I had no time to play—clearly the bus was seconds away from leaving without me. Reaching the bus, I climbed the steps panting and embarrassed, but glad to see my seat with my little plastic bag of snacks on it and my backpack on the shelf above it.

"We waited for you," said another passenger sternly as I passed him. I gave my best "gosh, I'm sorry, I'm such a goofy tourist, thanks for putting up with me" smile and said thanks, hurrying to plop down on the hard, dusty, semi-deluxe seat. I didn't want to fall over when the bus went tearing out of the lot trying to make up for the time I had cost everyone. I caught my breath and waited for the bus to take off, my only worry now where I would end up. We sat. My new friends stood under my window and waved to me. I waved back. We sat some more. The driver got off the bus and walked away. Weren't we supposed to be in a hurry?

After an interlude of bafflement on my part, the driver got on the bus and strode down the aisle toward me.

"Come," he said.

Wondering what I had done wrong, I grabbed my bag and followed him off the bus and across the lot. The little boy went back to his imaginary soccer game in front of me. "One rupee! One rupee! Hello, one rupee!" Another boy, even smaller and cuter and higher pitched joined in.

The driver led me to another bus. "This bus will take you to Gokarna," he said, gruffly but not unkindly. It was just as the station manager had promised—the driver would make sure I got to Gokarna. How could I ever have doubted it? I glanced around at the clamoring mill of people, the mingled woodsmoke and exhaust drifting past the green, red, and yellow busses. This must be Sirsi.

"Thank you," I said simply, knowing I couldn't convey all that I was grateful for. That no matter how clueless I was, the people around me knew what they were doing. And no matter how mistrustful I was, they were willing to help me. I gave each of the little boys a rupee and got on the new bus, which was exactly like the old bus, except for the curly script above the windshield that proclaimed its destination to everyone but me. The passengers all nodded at me as I passed them. I sat down in my new seat and saw all the kids outside my new window, the girls from the bathroom with the older one holding the baby, and the two little soccer boys, all grouped family portrait style and smiling big beautiful smiles up at me. Genuine smiles. They waved at me and I waved back, and they kept waving as my bus pulled out of the lot and onto the road to Gokarna.

Firmly convinced that buses are the way to travel, Megan Lyles has talked her photographer boyfriend into traveling with her by bus from New York City to Antarctica and helping her document the trip. (The final leg will have to be done by boat but that's not her fault.) You can follow along at www.meganlyles.com.

*

The first day I entered a public restroom in China I faced the ultimate toilet challenge. I had memorized the Chinese character for "women" to help minimize my anxiety. I would have figured this one out anyway, as next to the Chinese characters there was a picture of a high-heeled shoe for women and a cigar for men! My initial amusement turned to horror as I walked in and saw two rows of doorless stalls on raised platforms. I walked down the hallway with increasing levels of fear. I was distressed by the fact that the white ceramic "squat pots" weren't there. In fact, in their place was a long cement-lined trench that ran right through the stalls, from first to last, on both sides. Fear and confusion overtook me as I walked down the center aisle, trying to formulate my plan of attack. I knew I needed to squat, but the entire process was unclear to me. Do I straddle? What direction do I face? Why is there one long trench instead of individual bowls? What happens to the crap?

With trepidation, I pulled my pants down, placed one foot on either side of the trench and squatted, looking away from the hole. To my surprise, my neighbor's urine started flowing down the trench in my direction, headed for the hole beneath me! I quickly stood up, but of course I still needed to pee. I tried to squat and relax again, but the second I heard the sound of flushing from the toilet furthest "upstream," the entire plumbing system became shockingly clear to me! I jumped back up and watched in disbelief as this gush of water carried a ghastly pile of crap past me to the hole below my squat spot. I then realized that traveling in China was going to be challenging, amusing, and always an adventure.

—Konnie Landis, M.D., "Chinese Toilets 101"

* ✱ *

The Princess
and the Pee

Close-quarter combat takes on new meaning
to her highness.

ME, AN ADVENTUROUS TRAVELER? WELL, OF COURSE I like to think so. Sure, maybe not the kind that kayaks, canoes, or cavorts with local villagers in Third World countries, but I *am* willing to give up mascara for a week. I have also radically redeemed my pack-aholic ways of battering airport baggage scales with bulging suitcases closed only by application of ample butt pressure. The daredevil in me trusts I will survive our next vacation, a Windjammer Caribbean cruise, on only the barest of fashion essentials. Goodbye eveningwear, daywear, and five-extra-outfits-just-in-case wear—I'm now a one flip-flop pair, low-maintenance kind of gal!

Windjammers proudly proclaim to be the anti-cruise cruise ships. They eschew the frivolities of luxury liners, with their chichi cappuccino bars and tuxedoed attendants. Aye, instead prospective travelers are hooked by a pirate-like, devil-may-care voyage upon small, historically renovated ships decked in teak and sailcloth. Passengers are invited to help hoist sails, sleep on deck underneath the stars, or drink dinner away without ever slipping on the family jewels, or even a pair of shoes.

The glossy brochure guarantees that this is the trip for me:

> Windjammer shipmates are a motley crew of interesting folks from all over the United States and abroad. You won't know if the guy or gal sitting next to you is the CEO of a Fortune 500 company, or an Average Joe.

Well, O.K., even though this description encompasses everyone in the free world who can shell out the price of a ticket, I'm convinced I am one of those interesting, motley folks willing to forfeit plump pillows and Pérnod in favor of a genuine seafaring adventure. Yo ho ho!

I admit, however, I cannot conceal my trepidation concerning our bedroom quarters, particularly when we booked late and were issued what the brochure describes as a below-deck "Standard Cabin." I scan the description, believing I can make do without the in-room coffee maker, but am downright bewildered to learn the only accommodations worthy of mention are "upper and wider lower berths, private head and shower."

I can do this. I am The Adventurer.

To demonstrate my newfound flexibility, I assure my husband—who annoyingly doesn't seem to need any assurance—that our bunk beds are really a clever convenience—why, we can use the upper berth for extra storage space! From the particular angle in the brochure picture, the lower bunk appears wide enough for both of us. Maybe not like queen size-with-goose-down-filled-comforter wide, but surely large enough to accommodate late night snuggles.

It will be romantic—I am fairly certain.

We are greeted at a small pier in Saint Maarten by the cutest little launch boat that sputters us across the bay to meet the *S.V. Polynesia*. The 248-foot schooner stands regally against the blue velvet of evening sea. The weather is warm, balmy, and luxurious. To my surprise, I temporarily forget the havoc the humidity will wreak upon my hair. Instead, I whip out my brightest bandana and tie it over my head, handkerchief style, like the fashionistas I had spied upon in South Beach. I silently congratulate myself on copying this chic, but oh so casual, just-protect-me-from-the-wind style for my New Adventure Look.

The bed is smaller than I thought.

As promised, the bottom berth protrudes farther out than the top—but only by mere inches and I'm not sure what the architects had it in mind in offering this up. While the lower birth might more readily accommodate an obese person, or even a horizontal sexual act, I am certain it was never intended to sleep two adults, unless I imagine, those adults happened to be two medium-sized midgets who don't mind spooning.

"I get the top bunk!" my husband cries excitedly.

He is triumphant. As a boy growing up in a small apartment, his older brother always got the top bunk. Now, several decades and thinned hairs later, he feels avenged and is grinning with smug satisfaction.

Still, I am resolute, flexible, and flowing. Until I see the bathroom.

While I might have fallen for the sleeping under the stars schtick, they really pulled a good one over Adventure Girl by neglecting to mention that the bathroom is actually broom-closet-size, all-in-one shower, toilet, and sink. My husband marvels at the economy, noting he will be able to wash, urinate, and shave all at the same time. I, however, am noting the sensation of my behind pressed against a slick, wet toilet bowl while peeing. I am also sighing with a fond remembrance of the bathroom from last year's luxury hotel we snagged for a song on the Internet. While admittedly not nearly as efficient as the *Polynesia*'s accommodations, it did boast a sunken marble tub equipped with a remote-control television. Perhaps the playful, lurking threat of being electrocuted while flipping channels in the bubble bath is adventure enough for me.

With the wind slowly leaving my sails, I unpack while my husband christens the head with an inaugural whiz. As he finishes, we bump sideways past one another and I squeeze my extra large toiletry bag into the tiny, three-sided wire grid shelf hanging on the bathroom wall. While I may have been willing to forego makeup, it is downright ludicrous to think I might survive without my assortment of Clinique moisturizers and creams.

"Argh," I cry in my new pirate voice. The

——— ☽ ———

I was beginning to feel like the only woman in Egypt who wore out her underwear from both sides. I'd wear it right side out during the day, and turn it inside out for the evening. Sometimes, by the time I retired, I was afraid it wouldn't be dry by early the next morning. Each night, I'd anchor my bra and panties to the table on my balcony with ashtrays—hoping that the same breeze that was aiding them in drying wouldn't blow them over the balcony, and down the Nile.

◆

—Bonnie Mack,
"A Loaded Suitcase but
Nothing to Wear"

weight of my bag is too heavy for the little shelf and under
pressure it bursts away from the wall. The translucent, mesh-
clothed bag tumbles and plunks like a lead anchor directly
into the toilet bowl, which, in turn expels its water all over
the little broom closet bathroom floor.

Just as my quivering hand retrieves the bag, which is now
spilling liquid from inside-out all over my legs and feet, my
husband happens to mention he neglected to flush. I am no
longer that soft, cuddly Jack Sparrow of a pirate. I am
Blackbeard and I am out for blood.

"What do you mean you forgot to flush the toilet!" I
shriek, as this seems—at the moment—to be an act of in-
sanity on par with suffocating small kittens.

"It's a small ship and I wanted to help conserve water?"

On dry land, when I am not dripping in a puddle of
someone else's pee I might find this response endearing.
Instead I manage to use the word "fuck" ten times in one
sentence.

He promises that if I will just come out of the bathroom,
he will rinse everything with disinfectant, but I can't move.
I am paralyzed in pee.

"I am not coming out and tracking pee all over the car-
peting all over this room!"

"Well then let me come in," he pleads patiently, hoping
to placate a urine-soused lunatic.

"You can't come in. First of all, we probably both can't
fit in here, and second of all, then we both are going to
track pee."

"*Hon*," he sighs. Do I sense the weensiest bit of exasperation in his voice? "There is nothing wrong with *urine*. It is
completely sterile. There are people who actually drink
urine. There is even such a thing as *urine* therapy—you can
look it up on the Internet."

I can't stand the way he keeps referring to it by its formal name, like he is paying homage or something. And *therapy*? I have now lost all sense of rational thinking and am convinced that while I may be a crazy germaphobe, my husband has, at best, turned into a dead ringer for the Professor from *Gilligan's Island* and at worst, has been secretly participating in a satanic cult, drinking piping hot cups of urine while I was away at my Monday night yoga class.

I am wondering whether any of our Caribbean itineraries offer quickie divorces. I am spewing the "P" word uncontrollably. I am turning into Porky Pig with Tourette's Syndrome.

"W-w-well now what do you suggest? Should I just soak my contact lenses in your *p-p-pee*? And what about my cotton balls that are now drenched in your *p-p-pee*? How about if I just use your p-p-pee to cleanse my p-p-pores? In fact, why don't we dump out this whole bottle of Clinique cleanser and you can just re-p-plenish it with your miracle *p-p-pee*!!!"

Ever a man of patience, or perhaps soothed by years of drinking urine elixirs behind my back, my husband is finally able to convince me to sit down on the toilet as he lovingly and tenderly wipes the pee off my feet and rinses all of the contents of my bag in warm, soapy water.

To diffuse the mildly tense start to our vacation, or perhaps to avoid being held captive at sea with a madwoman for seven days, my husband suggests we quell rough waters with a trip above deck to snuggle underneath the stars. Begrudgingly, I agree. I am willing to forgive the watershed of our first evening, at least satisfied that I will have something to hang over his head for the rest of our married lives.

We grab thick rubber cushions off the lounge chairs and cuddle close under our woolen blankets. The gentle sway of the ship feels like a luxurious king-size waterbed and the zillions of luminescent stars winking in the sky are my personal pay-per-view movie. I am gently lulled to sleep in my husband's arms, dreaming of a cocoa-butter tan and sun-teased blond highlights that will be the envy of all my co-workers.

With each passing day, I am adjusting to my floating Winnebago lifestyle. Our cabin quarters have been transformed to a cozy, cool underground bunker after too many hours basting in the hot Caribbean sun. I am even enjoying my lower bunk. It is surprisingly refreshing to have a few evenings of respite from the fog of my husband's breath against my face. Still, I relish the comfort of having him near and knowing he is just one bed above me, sleeping in what I have affectionately dubbed "The Loft."

My inner pirate is thriving. I help hoist sails, drink more than my fair share of rum swizzles, and disco dance on Lingerie Night in teddy bear pjs, the cool, weathered teak floors tingling under my bare feet. Captain Casey, or just Casey, as he prefers to be called, commands the *Polynesia* with a charismatic blend of machismo and cutting comedy, salting his daily stories with expletives and edgy wisecracks that leave us in stitches. In keeping with his religious objection to formalities, he prefers baseball hats and tropical shirts to officer dress. One evening after sunset and swizzles, he sets up the floodlights and diving board so we can swim right off the side of the boat. It is an exhilarating experience, but when Casey suddenly grabs the ship microphone and bellows out to us, "Look out! Shark!… Just kidding!" my insides freeze for a nano-second, but then I am laughing hysterically. Life just shouldn't be taken so seriously, you know what I mean?

It is our last day at sea. As much as I am looking forward to resuming our conjugal sleeping arrangements, I'm also sorry to leave. Disco dancing will never be quite the same, and I'll miss Casey's antics and his most vigilant Windjammer edict "No whining!" which seems written expressly for re-covering prima donnas like me.

Later that night my husband awakens from a deep sleep needing to use the bathroom in a way that men of a certain age always do. Not wanting to wake me (perhaps still skittish from my minor proclivity to certain irrational tendencies), he gently closes the bathroom door behind him without turn-ing on the light, relieving himself in utter darkness. When finished, still semi-conscious with sleep, he blindly gropes and gives a hard turn to the doorknob, which to his horror, sends a shock of cold water exploding from the wall, dous-ing him from head to toe. Instinctively, he flinches and pan-ics, fearing the ship has sprung a leak, and is bursting a geyser of frigid water into our cabin.

It takes a moment before he gets his wits about him and realizes that in his bleary stupor, his hand has mistaken the knob for the door with the one for the cold shower spray and there will be no need for anyone to write a screenplay about our brush with a Caribbean iceberg. Meanwhile, I sleep soundly, dreaming equal parts rum swizzle, Johnny Depp, and golden doubloons.

As he recounts the story of his comeuppance to me early the next morning, I can only smile to myself at the discov-ery that even those without princess complexes are prey to the perils of small sailing vessels. I roll over in my lower bunk and fall back into a peaceful slumber, the gentle sea slowly rocking me toward home.

Julie Eisenberg lives in Miami, Florida. She and her husband Randy just bought their first fixer-upper boat, a twenty-five-foot trawler, which they plan to live aboard on weekends in the Florida Keys, once the mold-encrusted toilet, air conditioning, and 1970s orange-plaid uphol-stery are refurbished.

★

A tour group is not like family. A tour group is an endless, round-robin blind date. You utter the same information about yourself over and over and over again. By the eighth, ninth, kajillionth time you tell someone what you do and where you're from, you'll start making up stuff just to make yourself sound interesting—to your-self. I estimate I shared my personal data approximately one hun-dred times over the course of my travels. By the ninth rehash, I was telling people that I was a part-time rodeo clown and married to a rich, elderly Weimaraner.

—Mary Jo Pehl, "Your Tour Group and You"

MARCY GORDON

* * *

Gently You Have to Avoid a Frightening Behavior

It was an emergency in a foreign tongue.

LAST YEAR I DECIDED TO IMPROVE MY SCANT KNOWLEDGE of Italian and enrolled in a three-month intensive course at the Università per Stranieri in Perugia, the world-renowned language school for foreigners in Umbria, Italy. As part of the total immersion method, your first lesson starts in the basement of the university during registration week where you wait in line for hours with confused and disoriented people from all over the world—China, Japan, Germany, Taiwan, Russia, and Spain—with only one language in common—Italian.

While waiting in line for a permit of stay, I helped a completely bewildered Australian couple decipher their enrollment papers and informed them that they had been standing in the wrong line for the last two hours and then directed them to the registrar's office. Later, in another endless line, a girl from Japan wearing a Marilyn Manson t-shirt and a Hello Kitty backpack told me that Hello Kitty was *"in-ten-sho-no-lee i-row-nic."* Any previous doubts I had about Hello Kitty's intentions were now cleared up.

63

After negotiating the chaos of registration I received my student ID and could now eat for cheap in the student canteen as soon as I found out where it was. As I asked for directions, I noticed the Japanese girl, and the couple from Australia I had helped earlier, watching me intently. I set off for the cafeteria and all three followed me. I immediately jaywalked across four lanes of speeding traffic figuring I would lose them, but that only set in their minds that I was brazen and well versed in Italian culture. At the next intersection they caught up to me and I confessed I had no idea where I was going, only a vague sense of the general direction. The Australians said they didn't care where we ended up—they were just relieved to be with someone who spoke English.

They followed me down a steep dirt trail that led all the way from the top of the Mercato into an underground storage area where once our eyes adjusted to the dark we found three Ethiopians smoking a joint and unloading crates of lettuce from a service elevator. The three fellows quickly unloaded the remaining crates and left without a word. We decided to take the service elevator back to the top and as soon as the elevator doors closed we discovered there were no control buttons on the inside. Then the lights went out and the elevator began to move DOWN! Hello Kitty girl began to squeal like a pig to slaughter, which in turn caused the Australians to start laughing hysterically. When the doors opened we found ourselves deeper in the bowels of Perugia than seemed possible. Armed with my flashlight and some matches from the Aussies, we found a stairwell and climbed our way up towards the light. Six flights later we reached the top of the market, just a few feet from the dirt path where we had begun, and coincidently only a few yards from the cafeteria entrance. The Aussies, blessed with a robust sense of humor, appeared to have enjoyed the whole experience, but the Japanese girl seemed positively pissed. I guess she missed the non-intentional irony of the situation.

Over lunch I learned the Australians were both in their mid-60s, and had come to Perugia from Melbourne to take one month of Beginning Italian. Despite the fact they were speaking English, their heavy accents made it challenging to understand everything they said. She introduced herself as Grace and he gave his name as something that sounded like Attha. I thought it was African or Abo, and all through lunch I kept calling him variations on it like Attar or Atho and at one point I called him Aphid, like the bug. But it was not until Grace wrote down their names and phone number that I realized his name was Arthur, not Aphid.

Grace and Arthur told me the apartment they rented near the school had a kitchen full of pots and pans and other cooking utensils, but no dishes, cups, or eating implements of any kind. I joked that they should just borrow some items from the cafeteria to which Grace replied, "Capital idea!" and Aphid immediately began stuffing cutlery and plates into his backpack. After the heist, we decided to meet up later that evening and go to the movies. Grace and Arthur thought it would be a good way to immerse themselves in the language and culture without actually having to speak to anyone.

Much to our surprise the movie was not in Italian but in Korean with Italian subtitles. The film, from South Korea, was called *La Moglie Dell'Avvocato*, The Lawyers Wife...not the *avocado's* wife that Grace thought it meant. Anyway, talk about weird; it turned out the film was basically porn disguised as a highbrow South Korean soap opera.

From what I could piece together the story was as follows: Hojung is the frustrated wife of Mihjang, a successful lawyer who disses Hojung and takes up with his secretary.

Seeking revenge, Hojung gets involved with a very young guy—Wohung—who lives in her building. But things get complicated when Mihjang and his lover are killed in a car accident and Wohung's father discovers that his son is seeing Hojung and all hell breaks loose. I think it was a comedy. Aussie Grace thought the name of Hojung's lover was "well hung," which it did sound like and makes you wonder about the South Korean sense of humor. Arthur, a.k.a Aphid, slept through most of the show and spent the rest of the time pondering the possibility of swiping a stack of cold drink cups from the concession stand to augment their ill-equipped kitchen. I suggested he might as well take the popcorn maker, too, while he was at it, but he didn't think he could fit it in his backpack.

We continued to meet each day at the cantina between classes and fell into the kind of accelerated intimate friendship that is often forged among strangers when traveling far from home. The next week we saw another film, this time in German with Italian subtitles. Once again the story line seemed to be just the sheerest of veneers to host an all-out porn fest. It was rather surprising that all the films were distinctly adult in nature. I asked my host family about all the peculiar foreign films I had seen. They exchanged worried looks and explained delicately that the particular theater I'd been to was not exactly mainstream, but the "art house" for *experimental* films. I told Grace and Aphid I got the impression from my host family that we had been frequenting the local porn theater. Grace and Aphid were unfazed. Nothing rattled them. Aphid said it was all part of being Australian, that as a rule they tend to stay calm and not stress on the little things. I called their philosophy and attitude towards life—avoiding a frightening behavior—coined from a poorly translated fire emergency poster I saw in the cafeteria that read:

IN EVENT OF FIRE—GENTLY YOU HAVE TO AVOID TO ASSUME A FRIGHTENING BEHAVIOR.

I believe it meant "Relax, Stay Calm, and Don't Panic." Grace and Aphid always exuded an easy, relaxed air that I admired. But heck, they were on an extended vacation, with nothing really to worry about. Or so I thought.

Two days later things changed. At 3 A.M. I got a frantic call on my cell phone from Aussie Grace.

"Please come right away, it's an emergency," she said. "I'll explain when you get here."

Grace opened the door looking quite distressed and weary. Aphid was sitting hunched in the corner with a dishtowel in his lap.

"What is it? What's wrong?" I asked.

"It's Arthur it's…oh, how to say this…it's the prasta," said Grace.

"The what?"

"The prasta."

"The pasta? He ate something bad?"

"No, not the pasta, the prostata."

"Are you speaking English?"

"Yes, yes!" said Grace.

"Oh good God Grace," said Aphid. "Just tell her."

"Tell me what?"

"It's me little Joe…it's stuck," Aphid said.

"Your what? What the hell are you talking about?"

"Grace, give her the box," said Aphid.

Grace sheepishly handed me a carton.

"It's Viagra," Aphid said. "I took it several hours ago and…well…it went up but now it won't go down."

I burst out laughing and Grace started laughing, too. Aphid just moaned.

"Oh my God, I'm sorry," I said. "But what the hell do you want *me* to do? You Aussies are a kinky bunch. I'm not that kind of girl you know!"

"Oh please, be serious!" said Aphid. "We need you to read the box for us or help us call a doctor. We can't possibly explain this in Italian."

"O.K., O.K., let me see the package. Where did you get this stuff anyway and what were you thinking?"

"It's not that I *need* it," said Aphid. "We thought it would be fun to try—you can get it in the pharmacies here."

"Yeah right, I guess those foreign films put some ideas into your head."

Grace started laughing again.

"Marcy pleaseeee..." begged Aphid.

"You know I have to say that I'm really disappointed with you, this is so irresponsible, experimenting with drugs...and on a school night!"

"Please Marcy, read the package..."

"O.K....uh huh...uh huh...hmmmm interesting. All right then, lets try this—Aphid, stand up and put your hands over your head and stretch your fingers out as wide as you can."

"Will this help? Does it say to do that? What will this do?"

"Nothing, but you're always complaining that this flat needs a proper hat and coat rack—well, now you've got one."

Grace exploded with laughter.

"Oh please!" said Aphid. "This is not a joke, what does it really say?"

"I'm not a hundred percent sure but I think it says something about drug interactions and remaining calm. *Gently you have to avoid to assume a frightening behavior.*"

"What?" said Aphid looking puzzled.

"Never mind, it's a translation thing…"

Grace continued to laugh.

"Look Aphid," I said, "you need to relax. Grace, can you heat up some milk?"

"Warm milk? For what, a compress of sorts?" asked Grace.

"Oh jeeze no, I just thought it might be relaxing for him to drink."

"Oh right—brilliant—good idea," said Grace. "And then maybe we can give him some soothing thoughts—you know power of suggestion and all that—it could be beneficial for him to think of things that are *not* sexy."

"Things that are not sexy? That sounds like a *Jeopardy* category—I'll take things that are not sexy for $500!"

Aphid groaned and held his head in his hands.

"Well let's give it a try," said Grace. "Arthur dear, try to relax and concentrate on our words. I'll go first…how about…ducks?"

"Ducks?"

"Yes, ducks."

"O.K. how about…porridge?" I said.

"Oh yes, that's quite good, that's not sexy at all. My go. I'll say…flannel."

"Lentils."

"Hair-nets."

"Mustard."

"Tongue depressors."

"Salami."

"Salami?"

"Oh sorry," I said. "But I'm getting kind of hungry."

"Knee socks," said Grace.

We fired off words as if we were in the speed round of some demented game show.

But before I could give my next soothing thought, Aphid stood up and screamed—"For God's sake, this is ridiculous! Besides, actually I quite fancy knee socks. But nonetheless, I would like to go to hospital now."

At the hospital Grace and Aphid stood silently behind me as I tried to explain the exact nature of Aphid's problem. Although I was supposedly a Level II Italian student, my vocabulary was not equipped to convey all the details accurately. I couldn't recall the word for penis or even a slang term, so I made up words as I best I could to describe the situation:

"*Il poinger non va via. È va su e sopra ma no va giu.*"

"*Che cosa?*" What? asked the admission clerk.

"*Lui ha un grande problema con sua pee pee. Lui bisogna aiuto.*" He needs help.

I wondered if there was an international signal for "erectile distress" and what it possibly could be. In desperation, I resorted to hand gestures and began an elaborate pantomime. My impromptu floor show caused a sensation and everyone in the admissions area started laughing at what can best be described as a sort of Martha Grahamesque piece on fertility rites gone horribly awry. Eventually a doctor who spoke English was called down to see Aphid. *Il Dottore* took Aphid away and gave him some kind of shot and *il grande poinger* retreated.

Grace and Arthur returned to Melbourne with the majority of their dignity intact. But I was left to negotiate the streets of Perugia on my own, still too embarrassed to walk past the hospital for fear of running into anyone who might recognize me from my performance. I was trying very hard to *avoid a frightening behavior*, but it was going to take some time.

Marcy Gordon operates a marketing and publicity consulting firm, Bocca della Verita, which provides marketing services to travel guidebook publishers. She is a contributing editor to the new Authentic Tuscany series published by the Touring Club of Italy, which she also co-designed and developed in less-than-perfect Italian. Ms. Gordon spends unequal parts of the year in California and Italy. She is a graduate of the University of Florida College of Journalism and Communication with a degree in Advertising and Marketing.

* ✱ *

Paris, Third Time Around

But was it a charm?

THIS WOULD BE MY THIRD TRIP TO PARIS. THE FIRST time, my father escorted me on a trip organized by my eighth-grade French teacher. We stayed in a two-star hotel near the Gare du Nord. Every night, we ate omelettes, *frites*, and *mousse au chocolat* in noisy bistros, where the regulars discredited the myth of Parisian hauteur by engaging us in as much friendly conversation as our Midwestern-accented, academic French—mine current, Daddy's creaking with decades of rust—permitted. I had been given some early birthday presents to use on the trip: a straw purse, a high-collared trench coat that I considered far more feminine than the classic Burberry model, and some wood-soled sandals that attached via cream-colored, canvas ankle straps the width of fettuccine. I was, in a word, gorgeous: an eighth-grade woman of mystery in thick bangs cut to emulate *Mork and Mindy*'s Pam Dawber. The shop windows were bright with jonquils and chocolate molded into lambs, rabbits, and chickens. Unfortunately, the weather did not share the merchants' sunny Easter vision, treating me to my first taste of travelers' bane, the cold rain that pisses down from a pewter-colored sky for days on end. Freezing in my insubstantial off-brand trench coat, I clip-clopped from Notre Dame to Sacré Cœur, nearly breaking my tightly strapped ankles whenever my wooden soles hydroplaned on the wet cobblestones. I had a wonderful time, despite bunking with two ninth-graders who awarded themselves the choicest bathroom mirror time and both twin beds. I wheeled my rollaway cot next to our French (!) windows, dreaming of a not-too-distant future when I would return to this most romantic of cities with a handsome, artistically inclined man, temporarily played by whatever unsuspecting eighth-grade boy I felt like tapping for the fantasy. On my fourteenth birthday, the ninth-graders and I dressed up like French hookers and photographed each other posed seductively on my cot with Monsieur J. J., a worldly ten-year-old whose wealthy parents had sent him on the school-sponsored trip sans chaperone.

As I had predicted, the next time I saw Paris, I was in the company of a handsome, artistically inclined man, but, as shoestring travelers with only public facilities at our disposal, Nate and I were rank as goats. No doubt Paris has suffered its share of stenchy lovers. Napoleon and Joséphine come to mind. Juliette Gréco and Miles Davis had access to modern plumbing, but I'll bet they reeked of the bars in which they frisked. But with our constant stink further augmented by our poor diet, financial anxiety, and sleep deprivation, my libido didn't stand a chance of measuring up to the eighth-grade ideal.

This trip to Paris was different. Our digs in an old hotel off the Rue de Rivoli were fairly plush, food was plentiful, and this time I was wildly in love, flush with an infatuation as delicious and short-lived as the lone bead of nectar squeezed from a honeysuckle blossom. Unfortunately for my mother, she, not my lover, was my traveling companion. As soon as the Star gave her the green light, Mom invited me along, envisioning a fun mother-daughter escapade. We would arrive a week before Fashion Week, rent a car, and tour Normandy and the Loire Valley. At Giverny, we would picnic within spitting distance of Monet's infernal water lilies. Having glutted ourselves on the picturesque, we would roll into Paris, where we had a vague notion that I might tag along as a sort of barely fluent translator as Mom covered the collections.

Poor Mom. All I wanted to do was close my eyes and wake up in the cramped candlelit bedroom of the apartment my new boyfriend Wylie shared with two other architecture majors from the Illinois Institute of Technology. If Satan had materialized on the wrought-iron balcony, I would have swapped my mother and my soul for Wylie in a nanosecond. Mom knew it, but tried to keep a brave face. Just before we rendezvoused with our rental car, we were loading butter and marmalade onto uninspired croissants in our Paris hotel's basement breakfast room. A young couple seated themselves at the next table. The woman was pretty and blond, and the man, a tall Asian guy with a long ponytail hanging down his back, looked just like Wylie. I thought I would swoon. If only I could squat beside his chair, lay my palm on his back, and feel him breathing through the thin cotton of his shirt. That was all I wanted, just a crumb, a little morsel to tide me over for the next twelve days, the hundreds of hours I would be spending with my mother instead of Wylie. We watched the couple intently over the rims of our giant coffee bowls. Their voices were pitched too low for us to hear, but they held hands and smiled at each other frequently from inside their happy love bubble. "I'll bet you miss Wylie," Mom ventured, giggling uncertainly. Only 288 hours to go, I thought, not counting the return flight. I tore my eyes away from our neighbors, grunting an affirmative to my mother's question as I nonchalantly shook a Gauloise out of my pack. If I couldn't be with my lover, at least I could pretend to be French.

Under the cover of jet lag, I caught up on the many hours of sleep I had foregone since taking up with Wylie six weeks earlier. The humming of the rental car's wheels lulled me into unconsciousness, even as Mom freaked out from the pressure of confusing rotary exits and mileage signs posted in a language she didn't understand. These afternoon naps also served to transport me temporarily from the frenzied itching of a sudden-onset yeast infection, which, if nothing else, was expertly timed, given my transcontinental divide. Yeah, I was a real dud in the company department. Instead of lavishing me with admission to museums and gardens, and treating me to three provincial squares a day, my mother should have invited one of her friends, like Diney, her standing date for the Indiana Repertory Theater, or Ellen, a free spirit who painted watercolors of cows and Labrador retrievers. Either of those ladies would have been a livelier choice than I was, pining for Wylie's clove cigarettes and the red curtain he kept drawn across his bedroom window at all times.

Mealtimes were the hardest. In the car, I could sleep or twitch in my seat, trying to subdue the pernicious demons of my infection. Tourist attractions offered partial distraction from my Wylie-less state with their informational plaques, often helpfully translated into English. I learned quite a bit about the landing at Omaha Beach, the Bayeux Tapestry, Monet's love of Japanese woodcuts, and the monk-designed formal vegetable garden at the Château de Villandry. Sometimes I got pissy, like when Mom whispered to watch my bag as we passed through a street market en route to the famous cathedral in Chartres. When one is suffering from the pangs of lovesickness, the pragmatic comments of a mother cannot go unpunished. Only lovers think that they are immune from harm, that the whole world, even the tiniest forest creatures and most hardened criminals, wishes them well.

If I couldn't have Wylie, I longed for something to take my mind off him. As it was, I was afraid Mom and I were on the verge of turning into one of those long-married and almost universally feared elderly couples who dine silently in restaurants. After so long an acquaintance, what could we possibly say to each other over roast chicken and *vin ordinaire*? It didn't occur to me to ask Mom the same questions I had posed to Wylie in the breathless recent past, or that she, too, had plenty of anecdotes relating to a time before our paths crossed.

Back at our Right Bank hotel, we found our box overflowing with invitations to the designers' shows. My mother let me play with the stack, much as she used to let me do with the bridal announcements when I was nine years old, accompanying her to the Star on school vacations. My "job" was to stuff the posed studio portraits that had run with the Sunday bridal announcements into self-addressed stamped envelopes the young ladies had provided when submitting their nuptial information. (I don't want to alarm any soon-to-be-marrieds, but the staff had a long-running dog-of-the-week contest, which was both cruel and almost always easy to call.) In this spirit, I pawed through the designers' invitations, ridiculing the unestablished talents' attempts to lure the press with announcements printed on t-shirts, candy bars, and oversized, brightly colored cards that the hotel maid must have hated, since they leaked metallic confetti everywhere. My mother wasn't interested in these ploys. She raked through the pile, plucking out envelopes from the real players. Not every journalist who ventures to Paris makes the cut for the hottest shows' guest lists, so every big name came as a relief. "Oh, good, here's Ralphie," she said, pushing her red glasses higher on the bridge of her nose. (To the best of my knowledge, my mother's relationship with Ralphie does not extend beyond the labels in her denim shirtwaists and her approving opinions expressed in the *Indianapolis Star*. But there's an insider-speak that goes with the territory, and my mother is fluent in it.)

The invitations were for my mother only, but she had promised to try to secure a seat for me at a few shows, so I could check out the gibbering photographers screaming the top models' names in hopes of eye contact, the celebs seated ringside and the outlandish wedding gowns that are the grand finale of each designer's spring collection. "Oh, here's one at the Ritz," she mused, picking up a large square card edged in lipstick pink. "'The Paris Lip.' I have no idea who that is. Oh, look, it says Lauren Bacall is going to make some sort of presentation. I'll see if I can get you into that."

When I checked for mail, as I did several times a day, I wasn't hoping for late-arriving invitations. Every day thus far, I had sent at least one postcard to Wylie, covering it in tiny writing and kisses before slipping it into a yellow France Poste box. I calculated that mail between Paris and Chicago should have taken approximately a week. I grew increasingly despondent as each inquiry met with a courteous "Non, mademoiselle." My mother discreetly pretended not to notice. Why wasn't he writing? If he had written me the day I left, I would have had that letter upon our return from Normandy.

Our second night back in Paris, we woke to the unmistakable sound of enthusiastic, extended copulation. The acoustics of the airshaft were such that our neighbors' every gasp and groan reverberated with crystal clarity. We lay rigid in our beds, my mother and I, unable to ignore what was happening so bright, early, and close at hand. Wishing with all my might that the lovers would achieve a speedy, muffled climax, I couldn't help observing that at least someone was getting her money's worth out of a Paris hotel room. No doubt she was on her knees in an expertly hand-laundered garter belt and heels, expensively moisturized and maquillaged. She vocalized without inhibition, as people do when their mothers aren't within earshot. I wondered if she was a pro. "Sounds like a chicken," Mom observed grimly, staring at the ceiling.

Ayun Halliday is the sole staff member of the quarterly zine, The East Village Inky *and the author of* Job Hopper, No Touch Monkey!, *and* The Big Rumpus: A Mother's Tale from the Trenches. *She is* BUST *magazine's Mother Superior columnist and has contributed to* NPR, Hipmama, Bitch, Penthouse, *and more anthologies than you can shake a stick at without dangling a participle. Ayun lives in Brooklyn where she's allegedly "hard at work" on* Dirty Sugar Cookies, *a food memoir. Dare to be heinie and visit* www.ayunhalliday.com

OLIVIA EDWARD

* ✳ *

The Dangers of Going Local

*The author discovers that picking a Mandarin name
for herself in China can be a perilous task.*

"SO WHAT'S YOUR CHINESE NAME?"

"I haven't got one," I replied

"Well how can we print your business cards?" tutted the production manager impatiently.

"I don't know," I said limply. "I wasn't aware I was going to need one." Looks of disapproval and exasperation crossed the faces of my new Chinese colleagues.

I thought I'd done so well. Become one of those uber-cool global citizens I'd always wanted to be. Landed a dream job as a magazine editor in Shanghai. Found an apartment before I'd even set foot in the city. Arranged my flight and visa with minimal hassle. Said goodbye to my boyfriend and dog with minimal tears. Even managed to pick up a few words of Mandarin. And, yet, here I was, standing in my new place of work, only three hours off the plane, and I'd already made my first cultural faux pas.

Realizing I needed to get a name quickly, I asked what the other foreigners in the company had called themselves.

They reeled off a list of names translating into eulogies such as Tall Handsome One, Elegant Crane, Proud Butterfly, and Bringer of Light. Not even having had the chance to brush my teeth since landing, I didn't feel I was in any position to bestow such glorious compliments upon myself. My breath was stale and my hair looked as though I'd flown in from London strapped to the top of the plane.

It was explained to me that Chinese names were given by a child's parents or grandparents, in the hope of bringing them a bright future, but my sense of British modesty kicked in. I just stood there—international go-getter that I wasn't— shuffling from one foot to the other, until my assistant Happy came to my rescue.

"What's your middle name?" Happy asked.

"Amey," I replied.

"Well, that translates almost exactly into Chinese so that can be your name," said Happy, happily.

I'd always wanted to be Amey—Amey Andrews, after my mother's maiden name. And now I could be. New country, new name, new fabulous me. I smirked a little at the thought of my colleagues who had been arrogant enough to name themselves with praise and congratulated myself on my own choice of subtly glamorous moniker. Gratefully I signed a slip of paper confirming my authority for the printing, and soon had a box of name cards with my job title followed by my new name written in Chinese characters.

You're a nobody in China without a name card. On meeting someone new the first thing you do is swap name cards. I was soon sitting in meetings handing my cards out to fellow Chinese journalists, photographers, and high-flying businessmen. Often they would stop and repeat my Chinese name a number of times, pronouncing it *Ai-mee*, and check- ing to make sure they got it right. Then they would smile

slightly and emit an understanding "ah." Innocently I believed they were touched that a foreigner had so quickly picked up their ways.

Only a year later, after handing out over a thousand business cards, did I realize *why* they were smiling. It was as I was sitting in my Chinese language class, learning the correct forms of address for ordinary Chinese people—the man generally being *Xiansheng* and the woman being *Xiaojie* followed by their surnames—I was asked my name in order to incorporate it into a role play.

"*Aimee,*" I said with pride. "So I would refer to myself as "*Xiaojie Aimee.*"

The teacher sniggered. And despite his obvious urge to roll around on the floor, he managed to splutter, "Do you know what that means?"

"No," I replied with a sense of dread.

"*Ai* means love and *Mi* means rice. And *xiaojie* can also mean…" At this point the hilarity of the situation paralyzed him and a classmate had to help him out by kindly whispering the word "prostitute" in my ear.

Composing himself my teacher said firmly, "I think you better change your name, Miss Love Rice."

English writer Olivia Edward recently returned from Shanghai where she worked as editor-in-chief of travel magazine Voyage. *She has also contributed to numerous publications including the* Time Out, DK, *and* Luxe *guides, American Express magazines, and* Out Traveler. *She is currently writing the MTV guide to Ireland. Aside from words, she loves swimming in rough seas and drinking fresh watermelon juice.*

*

The best haircut I got in Ho Chi Minh City was at a salon called Krap. I'd been expat too long to notice the irony. Vietnamese often named their businesses after themselves, filling the street

with proudly lettered signs like Hoa's Noodles, Bich Flowers, and Pawn Shop Dung. For a year my daily commute had taken me past the My Thuat art gallery—against which the shock value of all other names seemed to pale. At least that's how I saw it. My housemate Andrew, from California, saw it differently.

"New cut?" he asked. "Where'd you go?"

"Korean place at the corner of Dong Khoi and Mac Dinh Chi."

"Hmm." Andrew's gaze stopped flitting over my hair and fixed abruptly on my face. At the corners, his lips began to twitch. "Black-and-white sign?"

"That's the one."

"KRA-A-AP! You went to KRAP!" He doubled over, hooting and gasping, skinny wrists flailing through the air.

Finally he sighed, wiping his eyes. "Did you get a card?"

I reached for my bag and pulled out the black-and-white business card. "KRAP by Parkseongchol," I read.

Andrew was back in hysterics.

—Mari Taketa, "The Search for Good Hair"

* ✱ *

Opera for Dummies

It was time to stop being jerked around.

IT STARTED WAY BACK IN 1978 WHEN I SAW *MAGIC*, THE Hollywood thriller starring Anthony Hopkins as a ventriloquist whose wooden dummy, "Fats," slowly goes crazy and embarks on a murderous rampage. The movie itself was terrifying. But it was the incessant airing of the TV commercial that really disturbed me. "Abracadabra, I sit on his knee," chanted the wide-eyed, high-voiced dummy while staring into the camera. "Presto-chango now he is me. Hocus pocus we put her to bed. Magic is fun. We're...dead."

O.K., maybe it doesn't seem so spine-chilling in print. But at the time, the movie and its ad were menacing enough to instill in me a lifelong fear of ventriloquists' dummies, marionettes and other small, hand-painted facsimiles of human beings.

I imagine myself rising from a warm bed at 2 A.M. to let the dog out only to encounter a Charlie McCarthy-type character seated serenely at my kitchen table in the moonlight. "I'm glad you're awake," he'd say, his stiff lower jaw clacking shut as his eyes dart, Kewpie-like, toward the gleaming butcher knife gripped in his white-gloved dummy hand.

For years, I've been able to get through most days without obsessing about the sinister potential of puppets. But recently I was in the Czech Republic, in Prague, where marionettes are allegedly part of a "long and rich tradition."

On my first day there, while walking through the narrow, cobblestone streets, I passed several shops selling the stringed puppets. Row upon row of still, expressionless marionettes hung limply from the walls, their hands and feet suspended in mid-air. There were rabbis and chefs and kings and witches, all of them silently beseeching passersby to give them life. I shuddered.

My friend Angela looked at me. "They creep you out too, huh?" she asked.

I nodded as I scurried past the shops.

That night at dinner, Angela and I discussed our jointly held fear of marionettes and other inanimate human beings. Sipping our wine, we talked as if we were discussing something semi-rational, like politics. "The problem I have with them is their inability to reason," Angela explained, using the highly logical lawyer's voice she typically reserves for closing arguments.

Yes, I agreed. That *was* one of their deficiencies.

"I mean, when they are attached to human beings, they're fine," she continued. "It's when they're left to their own devices that I have trouble with them." Angela, too, had seen the ads for *Magic*.

After dinner, we walked through Prague's old town and noticed, in the corners of lighted store windows, colorful posters advertising a production of *Don Giovanni* by the National Marionette Theatre. Instead of sleek ads for cigarettes, or posters promoting the latest action film like you'd see in other European cities, Prague was all about puppets. "No way," I proclaimed. Angela agreed, thus securing her position as my favorite traveling companion.

The next day we were led on a walking tour of the city by a Czech woman who alternated her talk between English, for us, and French, for the other couple on the tour. We'd stop in front of a Gothic cathedral and she'd spend twenty minutes talking excitedly with the French couple about, I assumed, the history of the church. Her hands would make wide swooping circles overhead, like she was describing the general craziness of church leaders during the Middle Ages. The French couple would nod their heads in rapid agreement. "*Oui, oui, oui, oui,*" they'd say, as if they were glad to have *finally* found someone who shared their passion for religious history. When it was time for the English version, the guide would turn to us and say something along the lines of: "This is the Teyn Church. Let's move on."

At one point, as I waited for the guide to finish a lengthy French narrative of the Charles Bridge, I spotted yet another marionette shop. This, in itself, was not unusual. What made this particular shop stand out was that its exterior speakers were broadcasting "Billie Jean" by Michael Jackson at levels loud enough to cause the last remaining communists in that city to pack their identical, government-issue suitcases and flee up the Vltava River. On the street in front of the shop, a small Pinocchio marionette in yellow pants was breakdancing, its red feet clomping on the cobblestones at the behest of the college-age salesperson controlling its strings.

"Look," I exclaimed before I knew what I was saying. "How cute!"

Angela stared at me as if I'd broken some unspoken covenant of the anti-marionette society. Then her eyes traveled to the breakdancing puppet. "They *are* less threatening when they dance," she conceded, a bit reluctantly.

With the edge taken off, we soon found ourselves admiring the range and artistry of marionettes available for sale. We discussed how marionettes could still be popular in a city that has survived the Habsburgs and communists, and now boasts sushi bars and Internet cafes. There must be *something* to this marionette business, we reasoned.

Our defenses crumbling, we scrambled for ways to keep our disdain of dummies intact. "The marionettes must just be for *tourists*," we scoffed. When that didn't work, we tried snobbery, ranking marionette theatre on the same cultural stratum as a monster truck rally.

But the more we questioned the allure of the puppets, the more we became fascinated by them. Over a beer and goulash that afternoon in a low-ceilinged Czech restaurant, Angela turned to me. "You know, I think we should see a marionette show, just to see what the fuss is about." I agreed, feeling strangely excited in a birthday party kind of way.

Back at the hotel we asked the desk clerk to make reservations for the following night. While she cradled the phone and waited for the theatre to answer, I sought confirmation for our decision. "Is it a *good* show?" I asked, eyebrows raised like a toddler seeking praise for a good deed.

The desk clerk sighed. She'd obviously heard this question a few thousand-million-jillion times before. "Yes," she said, the word ending in a slight "zee" sound. "It's nice, if you like the *Don Giovanni* music." Somehow, I wasn't reassured.

We arrived at the theater early the next night. Although advertised as a "beautiful hall decorated in Art Deco style," what we encountered was a sad, dimly lit theater with limp, red velvet curtains and green plaster walls the color of split pea soup. The walls had been gouged in several places, leaving white, dusty scabs. In the lobby, a pale young woman stood beneath a clothesline of cheap plastic marionettes, hoping for a sale.

When it was time for the performance to start, instead of subtly dimming the lights or ringing a low chime like they do for performances in New York, the National Marionette Theatre of Prague sounded something akin to an enormous school bell. Its insistent metal clapper reverberated painfully throughout the lobby. Startled, I didn't know whether to head to my seat, dart out the door for recess, or alert the captain that the sub was taking on water.

The show began, and the first marionette to appear was Mozart, who was dressed in pink satin with white ruffles at the neck and sleeves. He had curly silver hair that looked slept on, and his round wooden face bore a slight resemblance to Barbara Bush. As he jerkily "conducted" the imaginary orchestra—the real music was on tape—the other puppets made their appearance on the small stage. Controlled only by strings, they moved haltingly, like they were walking across a rope bridge in high winds. It was going to be a loooong night.

As the production got underway, my snootiness kicked in. The backdrops were painted in a style that could best be described as Scenery 101. I could see the thick hands *and* cleavage of several of the puppeteers. How unprofessional was *that?* I felt like I was watching a fifth-grade talent show where at any moment a little Indian girl would be tied to the stake while her parents clapped their enthusiastic approval. Most unsettling of all was that the marionettes' faces didn't move. At all. *Don Giovanni* maintained the same painted-on,

noncommittal expression regardless of whether he was se-
ducing the peasant girl Merlina or being engulfed by flames
for his evil misdeeds. It just didn't seem right.

Yet, despite myself, within a few short minutes I was
smiling, a silly what's-the-harm-in-this grin that lasted the
entire performance. I don't know if the grin appeared when
I realized that puppeteers are supposed to be part of the act.
Or when I realized that this particular production of *Don
Giovanni* was intended to be a comedy. Or when the Mozart
marionette drank too much wine and fell asleep, loudly
knocking his little wooden head on the edge of the imaginary orchestra pit.

Regardless, it dawned on me that the point of marionette
theatre is not to convince audience members that the puppets are real in an animated Hollywood kind of way. The
point was to give people an enjoyable, low-tech excuse for
listening to great opera.

When the performance was over and the puppeteers
emerged for their applause, it was clear from their pink
cheeks and broad smiles that they took immense pride in
their art form. I stood and clapped like a stage parent.

As we walked back to our hotel after the show, Angela
said, "I'm glad we're not like those people who don't try
new things because of fear or because they think something
is beneath them."

"Me, too," I said, gazing at the gold reflection of the city's
lights in the river.

"Sometimes, it just takes learning about something to
appreciate it," she reasoned, sounding like the host of a children's television show.

I concurred, thinking of all the times in my life I've passed
up opportunities because of fear, snobbery, or pre-conceived

notions. I thought about how often I've let closed-minded assumptions color my enjoyment of an event. I thought about how foolish many of my long-held, but unexamined, fears and judgments really are. Maybe *Magic* had been so scary because I was eighteen when I saw it and, frankly, a lot of my life was tinged with terror at that point.

As we neared the hotel, Angela made one final comment about the show. "You know," she declared, "those puppets didn't scare me *at all.*"

"Me neither," I said, secretly wondering if I'd have time at the airport to purchase a souvenir marionette.

Shari Caudron is a Denver-based writer whose work has appeared in Sunset, Reader's Digest, USA Today, *and other publications. She is also the author of* What Really Happened, *a collection of stories about the lessons life teaches you when you least expect it.*

. * .

His and Her Vacations

Think about it—Mars is cold and dusty,
Venus is hot and steamy.

THERE IS A DISPARITY BETWEEN WHAT WE (FEMALE types) think is a great vacation and what they (male types) think is a great vacation. Now, me, I think a cruise is just about your perfect vacation. One of the main selling points of a cruise is the time available for not doing Jack Shit. You can not do Jack Shit for the entire duration of a cruise. One reason is there is nothing that you can possibly need that is not on that boat. Add to that the staggering number of lackeys; as a passenger, you have at least twelve to fifteen of them assigned to you personally, and their sole reason for being is to prevent you from having to do Jack Shit. In addition, a whole covey of free-floating lackeys will come to your aid should your own personal set be out performing some other task for you when another urgent need arises—maybe a new umbrella for your drink. I do so love lackeys, and there are just hardly any at my house. Truth be told, there is only one—and she is me.

Another great thing about a cruise is the excellent food.

The first qualification for food to be excellent, in my book, is that somebody else prepare it, and all I have to do is show up and eat it. And there needs to be plenty of it—especially if other people want some of it, too. On a cruise, somebody else does all the cooking and apparently they do it round the clock because there is food everywhere you look, whenever you look. You can even order every single thing on the menu at every single meal and nobody will bat an eye. I love to do this because I always want to taste everything, and plenty of times I want to eat every scrap of it. But then, I am a notorious pigwoman....

What I'm saying is that the [Sweet Potato] Queens like vacations that are luxurious and pampering in nature, ones that involve lots of lolling about in lush surroundings. Guys, on the other hand, do not.

The following is an absolute true-life example of what can happen if you give a guy a bunch of money and a travel agent. It should provide all the proof you will ever need to support this ironclad rule: Never Let a Guy Plan a Vacation.

A good friend of mine recently returned (by the skin of his teeth) from a "dream vacation" that cost a gazillion and a half dollars. My friend Bill and his friend Ron put their heads together to figure out the farthest-away place that would cost the most *possible* money and time to reach, and would offer the *worst* accommodations imaginable, where they could go to and try to kill something big. Hmmm. How about Bearplop, Alaska?

So Bill and Ron coughed up big bucks and went to an inordinate amount of trouble to go to this godforsaken place in the nether regions of Alaska in order to hunt moose and grizzly bears. See, this is what the other women and I think qualifies this trip under the stupid category. Who of sound mind would go out of his way to try to have a confrontation with a grizzly bear? A guy, that's who. And clearly, a guy with not enough fiscal responsibility weighing him down. These guys have got that old problem (I never have it myself): You know what I mean, when you get too much money in your checking account, it will start backing up on you. You have to keep it moving freely through there in order to avoid the backup problem. When the money gets backed up, you resort to absurd measures to clear it out in a hurry.

Anyway, they have to fly for a couple of days to get to the part of Alaska that has people living in it, before they can head out to their forsaken vacation spot. *Forsaken* may be a misnomer; somebody would have had to live there in order to then forsake it, and I don't think anybody ever has or ever will live where these guys went. And don't you just imagine there's a good reason for that? I mean, look at Gulf Shores and Destin—you can't sling a dead cat without hitting a condo with a thousand people in it. That's because those are desirable locations. Where Bill and Ron went, you could sling a dead cat for a couple of thousand miles and not even hit a gas station or a mobile home park. Which, in and of itself, doesn't sound all bad, but the climate isn't exactly what you'd call a big draw. Y'know?

> M y mother buried three husbands, and two of them were just napping.
>
> ♦
>
> —Rita Rudner

Wheee! They are on the trek to their final destination, getting on progressively smaller airplanes at each leg of the journey, until finally, it is just Bill and Ron and the pilot in this itty-bitty plane which the pilot informs them is still too big to fly into where they're going. They land on this bald knob on top of a mountain and the pilot tells them to "get out and wait right here 'cause I'll be right back." And with that, he took off, leaving Bill and Ron on top of the bald knob with no food, no water, no nothing, including no idea when the pilot was coming back. Ostensibly he was going to get yet a smaller plane, but his parting words were no comfort to our intrepid travelers: "There's a tent in that box over there. You guys can put that up for shelter, in case I don't get back." Now, I *gotta* tell you, I'd have been stroking out big time. No way would I have let that guy fly merrily off into the wild blue yonder without my person being on that plane.

So Bill and Ron were stranded on the bald knob, somewhere in Alaska, and several hours later, the pilot returned, circled the knob, and flew away. This was perplexing to our heroes, a radio being high on the list of the things they did not have, along with food, water, shelter, guns, toilet facilities and/or paper. But by and by—then hours later—the pilot came back and landed, and took Bill away with him, with promises to Ron to "be right back." Happy Ron. "I'll be right back" is my all-time favorite line. And when *I* use it, what I really mean is: "Good-bye! If you're looking for me— I'll be the one that's gone! Just try and catch me! If I ever come back, it will be one chilly day, buckwheat!"

Eventually both made it to their vacation home, and were they ever happy then. "Home" was a Quonset hut on the side of what we in Mississippi would call a mountain or an Alp; the indigenous folk of Alaska liked to think of it as a "Hill." Meals would be taken "down the hill." And down the hill it was, too—300 feet straight down the hill. You practically had to rappel down three times a day. Meals were then followed by the inevitable climb back up the hill. Now, our boys were both in what I would call really good shape, but

nothing they had done here in the relative flatlands had prepared them for this "hill." For the first two days, they threw
up whatever meal they had just eaten, getting back up the
hill to the Quonset hut.

Remember, they came on this fire drill to hunt, specifically moose and grizzly bear. A fool's errand, if you ask me,
but, of course, nobody did. They hired "major-league hunting guides," who sound an awful lot like garden-variety
igmos to me. (But again, that is strictly my totally unsolicited
opinion.) In the whole two or three weeks they were stuck
off up there in the exact center of nowhere, how many
moose and/or grizzly bears do you think they saw? Well, let
me put it this way: I saw just as many in my very own backyard. "Hunting" with these wily woodsmen—these very expensive wily woodsmen—consisted of either (1) crashing
through the brush, making enough noise to alert every bear
and moose within a 200-mile radius, or (2) sitting by themselves on a stump, personally selected for them by their wily
woodsmen, for ten to twelve hours at a time. Sure makes me
want to take up huntin'. Boy hidee, it just sounds like a
bucket o' fun. I envision Bill and Ron off warming stumps,
while all the bears and moose were in the Quonset hut playing cards with the wily woodsmen....

But, as luck would have it, the pilot did, in fact, return for
Bill and he did, in fact, make it to the actual airport where
they have big airplanes. This brought up another issue. Out
in the wilderness, it was either unnoticeable or irrelevant,
but in the relative confines of the big airport, Bill could not
help but notice that he smelled like a goat, although perhaps
that reference is slanderous only to the goat and flattering to
Bill. Bottom line: he had not had a shower in a long time
and it showed—so much so that he himself could not bear
it. And so, as if it made perfect sense, he goes into the men's

room handicapped stall and strips. The man is completely naked in the men's room at the big airport, trying to de-funk himself with lavatory soap and wet paper towels. Quite a picture, no?

Several days late and somewhat scruffy, Bill did make good his return, amid great rejoicing by friends and family, who had no idea whether he would make it back alive or they would be claiming a box containing his stinky remains. All's well that ends well. Alaska is safe once more for the grizzlies and the moose.

If we were going to spend tens of thousands of dollars on a vacation, there would be things called "Sea Goddess" and "Ritz-Carlton" figuring prominently. Hell, we could have plastic surgery and recuperate in a fancy hotel for that kind of money. All we can think of is how very glad we are men don't try to make us go with them and how hilarious it is that they seem to think they are pulling something over on us by slipping off on these expeditions without us. We are laughing ourselves sick all the way home from dropping them off at the airport, are we not?

Here is the Queens' ideal vacation: Delbert McClinton's Blues Cruise. Delbert, as you may recall, is one of our very most favoritest musicians in the entire world, living or dead, and he sponsors a cruise every January and books all the rest of our very most favoritest musicians in the entire world, living or dead, to go on this cruise with him. They all perform just night and day the whole time, so you can be on a cruise, getting waited on hand and foot, basking in the sun, even seeing exotic ports of call if you're so inclined. (But I warn you, the lackeys do not follow you ashore to wait on you hand and foot there.) You can have all this *plus* you get to dance with Delbert and his buddies all night every night. I cannot imagine a circumstance under which you could possibly have more fun unless you happen to own a monkey that I don't know anything about.

For all you Wannabe Wannabes out there who have been clamoring for a Sweet Potato Queen Convention, here's the deal: We're all going on Delbert's Blues Cruise! All you have to do—I'm completely serious—is call this number: 1-800-DELBERT and tell them you want to book yourself and your cohorts for a week of Sweet Potato Queens and Delbert. Don't bother paying your bills before you leave—you won't be wanting to go home, anyway.

Jill Conner Browne, royal boss of Jackson, Mississippi's own glorious Sweet Potato Queens, introduced them to the world in the bestseller The Sweet Potato Queen's Book of Love. *She is also the author of the bestselling* The Sweet Potato Queens' Financial Planner *and* God Save the Sweet Potato Queens, *from which piece was excerpted.*

KATIE McLANE

* ✳ *

The Yellow Lady

I'll have what she's having, bartender.

PAINTED WITH WHAT LOOKED MORE LIKE BROWN sludge than paint, the sign stated proudly:

> Don Chongs Camping
> Camp by River
> $3 US a night

Dust flew up around me as I made my way under the fronds of towering date trees, ripe with clusters of their sweet oblong fruit. Eagles circled above, serenading me with the rustling of their wings. Nestled amongst the palms, I found a spot near a sandy beach to unpack my things and establish my new home. Little did I know that near this oasis town of San Ignacio on the Baja peninsula, I was about to find an elixir that would change my life. Well, at least alter my way of thinking for a few hours.

In town, an immense eighteenth-century Catholic Church loomed above me. Locals loitered in the small plaza. Trailers selling fish tacos littered the streets. A liquor store occupied the corner, and when I entered all talking stopped. The weathered Mexican men turned to stare. They whispered. They laughed. I went about my business, wishing I had learned more Spanish before embarking on my journey.

"You just *have* to try the yellow lady liqueur, Kate," some friends suggested before I left home.

"Yellow lady?" I asked.

Even though they could not remember the exact name of it, they assured me that I had to try it. I searched the dusty, whitewashed shelves. No yellow lady was to be found. As I turned to walk out of the store, I spotted a bottle shaped like a thick-bodied woman, hands resting on her swollen belly. Filled with a gleaming yellow liquid, she shimmered as the sun from the windows hit her full breasts.

The bottle was high on a shelf. I couldn't reach her. I took a deep breath, tried the little Spanish I knew, and asked the old man behind the counter for help. He sighed and meandered towards me.

I pointed at the bottle.

He smiled. Then he breathed, "Damiana."

"Damiana?" I asked.

He smiled and winked at me as we walked to the register.

"Ooohhhhh, Damiana!" cried his friends when they spotted my bottle. Each one slapped me on my back, chuckling, as I left the store.

I arrived back at camp and slowly poured some of the glimmering, flaxen liqueur in a shot glass, a little leery after the men's reaction. The liquid was sweet, smooth, and went down easy. Don Chong, in work boots and faded blue jeans, sauntered through the palms. His graying sideburns and mustache stood out against his olive skin. He flashed a sweet smile as he eyed my bottle. We chatted, and soon he put his arm around me and sat close. His friendly advances worried me, so I told him that I was turning in and bid him *adios*.

The next day I drove south to a fishing village called Mulege. A dusty dirt road led me down to a small beach with cappuccino-colored sand, a dollop of froth on its rim from the spray of the turquoise sea. I rented a *palapa* for $3 a night. Made from dried palm leaves stretched across frail poles, this three-sided shack was a perfect shelter from the hot after-noon sun.

On a *palapa* near mine a dozen small paintings were hung. Underneath them, a young blonde woman sat at a table painting another work of art. I looked over her shoulder and watched as the image of a worn collapsing building began to appear, revealing the decay and disintegration of an other-wise solid structure. She had frozen the moment in time, and her out-of-slant perspective made the scene look somewhat psychedelic. She kept looking up to study her subject when I realized she was painting the outhouse.

"¿El cuarto de baño?" I asked.

She smiled and nodded. "Hi, I'm Lorna."

"Nice to meet you, can I offer you a drink?"

"What, is it?" she asked as she eyed my bottle.

"I'm not sure, but it's real good," I confessed.

"You've had some?"

"Oh, yeah!"

After a little coaxing, she said she would try it.

I poured us both a drink, and went to use *el baño*. As I walked back to our makeshift cantina in the sand, I saw Lorna trying to generate enough courage to take a drink. She picked up and looked at the bottle, sniffed the glass, and finally took a feeble, tiny taste. She smiled, and then took one long, slow swallow and it was gone. Suddenly, the manager of the *palapas* was at her side. Pablo, with a white cowboy hat covering his eyes, and short-sleeved plaid shirt, buttons bursting at his paunch, kept smiling his lusty smile at her. Although the language barrier made it hard for them to have a conversation, he was persistent.

She glanced at me, her eyes pleading, "Help me." I asked if she wanted to walk to town. With an enthusiastic "Yes!" she followed me, thanking me profusely.

"What got into him all of a sudden?" Lorna wondered out loud.

"I don't know, but there seems to be a lot of it going around lately!"

Arriving in town, we pulled the yellow lady out of my daypack, and took a couple of big swigs. We walked into the small, dingy corner store, the top of the bottle sticking out of my bag. A short, dark-skinned, wrinkled man walked up to us and smiled.

"Pedro, Kissy Pedro," he said, jutting his weathered hand out for us to shake. He might have been eighty or maybe just sixty and had led a hard life. We smiled back, it was hard not to, looking at his infectious, toothless grin. His hands had a permanent shake to them, but the gleam in his eye when he smiled at us was that of a twenty-year-old man.

Lorna rolled her eyes and groaned, "Oh brother, not another one!"

When we left the store, Kissy Pedro was right behind us with bloodshot eyes, quivering voice, and big black holes in place of bicuspids. We came to an intersection. Pedro insisted on helping us. He held out two boney elbows and we grabbed on. Behind us, Kissy Pedro's friends watched as he took two American women across the street. Lorna winked at me, and gave him a kiss on the cheek for all his friends to see. I followed suit. Cries and catcalls came from the men on the corner. Pedro smiled, then pulled me down to his level and tried to stick his tongue down my throat. I leaped away, grabbed Lorna's arm, and we ran, laughing all the way back to our *palapas*.

In the morning, I stood on the beach in the magenta hue of dawn. A ruby brilliance shone over the horizon and reflected onto the water. The uppermost reaches of the sky were crimson and cobalt, the shoreline dark. A lone boat was out at sea; the silhouette of a single fisherman added a feeling of tranquility to the scene. Suddenly, the warmth of two muscular arms wrapped around me. I spun around. There was Jonathan, a man I had longed for since I first laid eyes on him years earlier.

"What are you doing here? How did you find me?"

He pressed his finger to my lips to silence me. He carried me into the water where we met the colors of the sunrise. Our wet bodies trembled as one in the sea. He kissed me gently, working his way down the nape of my neck. As he reached the silky fabric of my blouse, I awoke to the most God-awful, slobbering, mangy dog in my hammock, smelling like he had rolled in something that crawled out from the bottom of the sea and died. You could see his green breath with every forceful pant.

After a night of fitful sleep, filled with more wild erotic dreams, I just had to find out what was in the yellow lady. As I explored the town that day, I asked shopkeepers, bartenders, everyone. All they would say was "Damiana," and then they would smile, nod, and wink. Finally a waiter added to the mystery. "Ahhhh, the Love Liqueur" was all he said.

Determined to find out the truth, I found the tag that came tied around the neck of the bottle. I brought out my "Spanish-English" dictionary, my "English-Spanish" dictionary, my *Spanish for Travelers in Mexico* book, my *Everything You Need to Know While Travelling in Baja* book, and the electronic translator I had purchased for times such as these. I looked up every word on that tag.

Two of the Spanish words were not in any of the books. When I entered them into the little electronic brain however, the words "powerful aphrodisiac" popped up. It all came rushing back to me, Don Chong, Pablo, Pedro, and all those dreams.

Oh, those dreams.

Katie McLane was born in Cambridge, England, and now lives in the Pacific Northwest on her thirty-two-foot sailboat, moondance. *When she is not sailing about the San Juan Islands, she is working on her first book,* 2000 Tides.

★

After lunch, I headed back to the air-conditioned luxury of the tour bus to await the trip back to Cancún. The driver and I were the only people on the bus. I asked him, "*¿Habla inglés?*" He didn't speak English, so we tried to converse in Spanish. Let me rephrase that. I tried. He, on the other hand, had a perfectly good grasp of his native language. We exchanged pleasant hellos. Then he, like every male I'd come across in Mexico thus far, complemented me on my *amarillo* hair. I was a yellow-blonde on that first trip to Mexico, and on my first day there I had felt like the most beautiful woman in the world because the men were much more attentive to me than those in my home country of Canada. I thanked the bus driver, who then said something that I did not understand. He then did something quite strange; he pulled down the zipper on his pants! I'm not quite sure if he was trying to show me that the hair on his carpet matched that of his attic, but all I could think of saying was, "*¡No entiendo!*" That ended that conversation, and the zipper went back up. I never felt I was in any danger, but to this day, I still wonder which of my Spanglish he mistook for, "Please undo your pants for me, Señor Bus Driver."

—Louise Schutte, "Spanglish and Me"

SUSAN ORLEAN

. ✦ .

Lifelike

Honey, what's that in the freezer?

AS SOON AS THE 2003 WORLD TAXIDERMY CHAMPION-
ships opened, the heads came rolling in the door. There were
foxes and moose and freeze-dried wild turkeys; mallards and
buffalo and chipmunks and wolves; weasels and buffleheads
and bobcats and jackdaws; big fish and little fish and razor-
backed boar. The deer came in herds, in carloads, and on pal-
lets: dozens and dozens of whitetail and roe; half deer and
whole deer and deer with deformities, sneezing and glower-
ing and nuzzling and yawning; does chewing apples and
bucks nibbling leaves. There were millions of eyes, boxes and
bowls of them, some as small as a lentil and some as big as a
poached egg. There were animal mannequins, blank faced
and brooding, earless and eyeless and utterly bald: ghostly
gray duikers and spectral pine martens and black-bellied tree
ducks from some other world. An entire exhibit hall was
filled with equipment, all the gear required to bring something dead back to life: replacement noses for grizzlies, false
teeth for beavers, fish-fin cream, casting clay, upholstery nails.

The championships were held in April at the Springfield, Illinois, Crowne Plaza hotel, the sort of nicely appointed place that seems more suited to regional sales conferences and rehearsal dinners than to having wolves in the corridors and people crossing the lobby shouting, "Heads up! Buffalo coming through!" A thousand taxidermists converged on Springfield to have their best pieces judged and to attend such seminars as "Mounting Flying Waterfowl," "Whitetail Deer—From a Master!," and "Using a Fleshing Machine." In the Crowne Plaza lobby, across from the concierge desk, a grooming area had been set up. The taxidermists were bent over their animals, holding flashlights to check problem areas like tear ducts and nostrils and wielding toothbrushes to tidy flyaway fur. People milled around, greeting fellow taxidermists they hadn't seen since the world championships, held in Springfield two years ago, and talking shop.

"Acetone rubbed on a squirrel tail will fluff it right back up."

"My feeling is that it's quite tough to do a good tongue."

"The toes on a real competitive piece are very important. I think Bondo works nicely, and so does Super Glue."

"I knew a fellow with cattle, and I told him, 'If you ever have one stillborn, I'd really like to have it.' I thought it would make a really nice mount."

That there is a taxidermy championship at all is something of an astonishment, not only to the people in the world who have no use for a Dan-D-Noser and Soft Touch Duck Degreaser, but also to taxidermists themselves. For a long time, taxidermists kept their own counsel. Taxidermy, the three-dimensional representation of animals for permanent display, has been around since the eighteenth century, but it was first brought into popular regard by the Victorians, who thrilled to all tokens of exotic travel and especially to any domesticated representations of wilderness—the glassed-in miniature rain forest on the tea table, the mounted antelope by the front door. The original taxidermists were upholsterers who tanned the hides of hunting trophies and then plumped them up with rags and cotton, so that they reassumed their original shape and size; those early poses were still and simple, the expressions fairly expressionless. The practice grew popular in this country, too: by 1882, there was a Society of American Taxidermists, which held annual meetings and published scholarly reports, especially on the matter of preparing animals for museum display. As long as taxidermy served to preserve wild animals and make them available for study, it was viewed as an honorable trade, but most people were still discomfited by it. How could you not be? It was the business of dealing with dead things, coupled with the questionable enterprise of making dead things look like live things. In spite of its scientific value, it was usually regarded as almost a black art, a wholly owned subsidiary of witchcraft and voodoo. By the early part of the twentieth century, taxidermists such as Carl E. Akeley, William T. Hornaday, and Leon Pray had refined techniques and begun emphasizing artistry. But the more the techniques of taxidermy improved, the more it discomfited: Instead of the lumpy moose head that was so artless that it looked fake, there were mounts of pouncing bobcats so immaculately and exactly preserved, they made you flinch.

For the next several decades, taxidermy existed in the margins—a few practitioners here and there, often self-taught and usually known only by word of mouth. Then, in the late 1960s, a sort of transformation began: the business started to seem cleaner and less creepy—or maybe, in that messy, morbid time, popular culture started to again appreciate the messy, morbid business of mounting animals for display. An ironic reinterpretation of cluttered, bourgeois

Victoriana and its strained juxtapositions of the natural and the man-made was in full revival—what hippie outpost didn't have a stuffed owl or a moose head draped with a silk shawl?—so, once again, taxidermy found a place in the public eye. Supply houses concocted new solvents and better tanning compounds, came out with lightweight mannequins, produced modern formulations of resins and clays. Taxidermy schools opened; previously, any aspiring taxidermist could hope to learn the trade only by apprenticing or by taking one of a few correspondence courses available. In 1971, the National Taxidermy Association was formed (the old society had moldered long before). In 1974, a trade magazine called *Taxidermy Review* began sponsoring national competitions. For the first time, most taxidermists had a chance to meet one another and share advice on how to glue tongues into jaw sets or accurately measure the carcass of a squirrel.

The competitions were also the first time that taxidermists could compare their skills and see who in the business could sculpt the best moose septum or could most perfectly capture the look on a prowling coyote's face. Taxidermic skill is a function of how deft you are at skinning an animal and then stretching its hide over a mannequin and sewing it into place. Top-of-the-line taxidermists sculpt their own mannequins; otherwise they will buy a ready-made polyurethane foam form and tailor the skin to fit. Body parts that can't be preserved (ears, eyes, noses, lips, tongues) can be either store-bought or hand-made. How good the mount looks—that is, how alive it looks—is a function of how assiduously the taxidermist has studied reference material (photographs, drawings, and actual live animals) so that he or she knows the particular creature literally and figuratively inside out.

To be good at taxidermy, you have to be good at sewing,

sculpting, painting, and hairdressing, and mostly you have to be a little bit of a zoology nerd. You have to love animals— love looking at them, taking photographs of them, hunting them, measuring them, casting them in plaster of Paris when they're dead so that you have a reference when you're, say, attaching ears or lips and want to get the angle and shape exactly right. Some taxidermists raise the animals they most often mount, so they can just step out in the backyard when they're trying to remember exactly how a deer looks when it's licking its nose, especially because modern taxidermy emphasizes mounts with interesting expressions, rather than the stunned-looking creations of the past. Taxidermists seem to make little distinction between loving animals that are alive and loving

——— ☽ ———

Not long after our arrival in England, a fellow American student developed a hankering for fried chicken while riding the London Underground.

Silently giving thanks for the abundance of fast-food establishments dotting London, she resolved to ask the first person she saw where she might find a Kentucky Fried Chicken.

Stepping off the train, she saw a woman handing out tracts. As the woman pressed one into her hand, my friend asked eagerly, "Excuse me, where is the nearest Kentucky Fried Chicken?"

The woman's pleasant expression quickly changed to one of shock and disgust.

My friend looked down at the tract in her hand. It began, "Each day, thousands of chickens are needlessly slaughtered to satisfy the gluttony of man…"

◆

—Carol Penn-Romine,
"Tastes of Home"

ones that are not. "I love deer," one of my champions in the Whitetail division said to me. "They're my babies."

Taxidermy is now estimated to be a $570 million annual business, made up of small operators around the country who mount animals for museums, for decorators, and mostly for the 13 million or so Americans who are recreational hunters and on occasion want to preserve and display something they killed and who are willing to shell out anywhere from two hundred dollars to mount a pheasant to several thousand for a kudu or a grizzly bear. There are state and regional taxidermy competitions throughout the year; two trade magazines; a score of taxidermy schools; and 3,000 visits to Taxidermy.net every day, where taxidermists can trade information and goods with as little self-consciousness as you would find on a knitting website:

> "I am in need of several pair of frozen goat feet?"
>
> "Hi! I have up to three hundred sets of goat feet and up to one thousand sets of sheep feet per month. Drop me an email at frozencritters.com...or give me a call and we can discuss your needs."
>
> "I have a very nice small raccoon that is frozen whole. I forgot he was in the freezer. Without taking exact measurements I would guess he is about twelve inches or so—very cute little one. Will make a very nice mount."
>
> "Can I rinse a boar hide good and freeze it?"
>
> "Bob, if it's salted, don't worry about it!"
>
> "Can someone please tell me the proper way to preserve turkey legs and spurs? Thanks!"
>
> "Brian, I inject the feet with Preservz-It...Enjoy!"

The word in the grooming area was that a piece to beat was Chris Krueger's happy-looking otters swimming in a perpetual circle around a leopard frog. A posting on Taxidermy.net earlier in the week declared, "EVERY-THING about this mount KICKS BUTT!!" Kicking butt, in this area of taxidermy, requires having a mount that is not just lifelike but also artistic. It used to be enough to do what taxidermists call "fish on a stick" displays; now a serious competitor worries about things like flow and negative space and originality. One of this year's contenders, for instance, Ken Walker's giant panda, had artistry and accuracy going for it, along with the element of surprise. The thing looked a hundred percent pure panda, but you can't go out and shoot a panda, and you aren't likely to get hold of a panda that has met a natural end, so everyone was dying to know how he had done it. The day the show opened, Walker was in the grooming area, gluing bamboo into place behind the animal's paws, and a crowd had gathered around him. Walker works as a staff taxidermist for the Smithsonian. He is a breezy, shaggy-haired guy whose hands are always busy. One day, I saw him holding a piece of clay while waiting for a seminar to begin, and within thirty seconds, or so, without actually paying much attention to it, he had molded the clay into a little minklike creature.

"The panda was actually pretty easy," he was saying. "I just took two black bears and bleached one of them—I think I used Clairol Basic. Then I sewed the two skins together into a panda pattern." He took out a toothbrush and fluffed the fur on the panda's face. "At the world championship two years ago, a guy came in with an extinct Labrador duck. I was in awe. I thought, What could beat that—an extinct duck? And I came up with this idea." He said he thought that the panda would get points for creativity alone. "You can score a ninety-eight with a squirrel, but it's still a squirrel," he said. "So that means I'm going with a panda."

"What did you do for toenails, Ken?" Someone asked.

"I left the black bear's toenails in," he said. "They looked pretty good."

Another passerby stopped to admire the panda. He was carrying a grooming kit, which appeared to contain Elmer's glue, brown and black paint, a small tool set, and a bottle of Suave mousse. "I killed a blond bear once," he said to Ken. "A two-hundred-pound sow. Whew, she made a beautiful mount."

"I'll bet," Ken said. He stepped back to admire the panda. "I like doing re-creations of these endangered animals and extinct animals, since that's the only way anyone's going to have one. Two years ago, I did a saber-toothed cat. I got an old lioness from a zoo and bleached her."

The panda was entered in the Re-Creation (Mammal) division, one of the dozens of divisions and subdivisions and sub-subcategories, ranging from the superspecific (Whitetail Deer Long Hair, Open Mouth division) to the sweepingly colossal (Best in World), that would share in twenty-five thousand dollars' worth of prizes. (There is even a sub-sub-subspecialty known as "fish carving," which uses no natural fish parts at all; it is resin and wood sculpted into a fish form and then painted.) Nearly all the competitors are professionals, and they publicize their awards wherever possible. For instance, instead of ordering just any Boar Eye-Setting Reference Head out of taxidermy catalog, you can order the Noonkester's #NRBERH head sculpted by Bones Johnson, which was, as the catalog notes, the 2000 National Taxidermy Association Champion Gamehead.

The taxidermists take the competition very seriously. During the time I was in Springfield, I heard conversations analyzing such arcane subjects as exactly how much a javelina's snout wrinkles when it snarls and which molars deer use to chew acorns as opposed to which ones they use to chew leaves. This is important because the ultimate goal of a taxidermist is to make the animal look exactly as if it had never died, as if it were still in the middle of doing ordinary animal things like plucking berries off a bush or taking a nap. When I walked around with the judges one morning, I heard discussions that were practically Talmudic, about whether the eyelids on a particular bison mount were overdetailed, and whether the nostrils on a springbok were too wide, and whether the placement of whiskers on an otter appeared too deliberate. "You do get compulsive," a taxidermist in the exhibit hall explained to me one afternoon. At the time, he was running a feather duster over his entry—a bobcat hanging off an icicle-covered rock—in the last moments before the judging would begin. "When you're working on a piece, you forget to eat, you forget to drink, you even forget to sleep. You get up in the middle of the night and go into the shop so you can keep working. You get completely caught up in it. You want it to be perfect. You're trying to make something come back to life."

I said that his bobcat was beautiful and that even the icicles on the piece looked completely real. "I made them myself," he said. "I used clear acrylic toilet plunger handles. The good Lord sent the idea to me while I was in a hardware store. I just took the handles and put them in the oven at four hundred degrees." He tapped the icicles and then added, "My wife was pretty worried, but I did it on a nonstick cookie sheet."

So who wants to be a taxidermist? "I was a meat cutter for fifteen years," a taxidermist from Kentucky said to me. "That whole time, no one ever said to me, 'Boy, that was a wonderful steak you cut me.' Now I get told all the time what a great job I've done." Steve Faechner, who is the president and chairman of the Academy of Realistic Taxidermy, in Havre, Montana, started mounting animals in 1989, after years spent working on the railroad. "I had gotten hurt and was looking for something to do," he said. "I was with a friend who did taxidermy and I thought to myself, I have got to get a life. And this was it." Larry Blomquist, who is the owner of the World Taxidermy Championships and of *Breakthrough*, the trade magazine that sponsors the competition, was a schoolteacher for three years before setting up his business. There are a number of women taxidermists (one was teaching this year's seminar, "Problem Areas in Mammal Taxidermy"), and there are budding junior taxidermists, who had their own competition division, for kids fourteen and younger, at the show.

The night the show opened, I went to dinner with three taxidermists who had driven in from Kentucky, Michigan, and Maryland. They were all married, and all had wives who complained when they found one too many antelope carcasses in the family freezer, and all worked full-time mounting animals—mostly deer for local hunters, but occasional safari work for people who had shot something in Africa. When I mentioned that I had no idea that a person could make a living as a taxidermist, they burst out laughing, and the guy from Kentucky pointed out that he lived in a little town and there were two other full-time taxidermists in business right down the road.

"What's the big buzz this year?" the man from Michigan asked.

"I don't know. Probably something new with eyes," the guy from Maryland answered. "That's where you see the big advances. Remember at the last championship, those Russian eyes?" These were glass animal eyes that had a reflective paint embedded in them, so that if you shone a light, they would shine back at you, sort of like the way real animals' eyes do. The men discussed those for a while, then talked about the new fish eyes being introduced this year, which have photographic transfers of actual fish eyes printed on plastic lenses. We happened to be in a restaurant with a sports theme, and there were about a hundred televisions on around the room, broadcasting dozens of different athletic events, but the men never glanced at them and never stopped talking about their trade. We had all ordered barbecued ribs. When dinner was over, all three of them were fiddling around with the bones before the waitress came to clear our plates.

"Look at these," the man from Kentucky said, holding up a rib. "You could take these home and use them to make a skeleton."

Susan Orlean is the bestselling author of The Orchid Thief *(which was the inspiration for the film* Adaptation*),* The Bullfighter Checks Her Makeup, *and* Saturday Night. *She has been a staff writer at* The New Yorker *since 1992. Her articles have also appeared in* Outside, Rolling Stone, Vogue, *and* Esquire. *She lives in New York City with her husband, John Gillespie. This piece was excerpted from* My Kind of Place: Travel Stories from a Woman Who's Been Everywhere. *For more information, go to www.susanorlean.com.*

ANASTASIA M. ASHMAN

* * *

My Husband Is Lost Without Me

The master of the road takes a new mistress.

MOST OF THE TIME MY HUSBAND AND I WORK AS A complementary team. He trusts my research skills and intuition to invest money and choose gifts for his mother; I defer to his computational and engineering strengths with taxes and misbehaving electronics. At home in New York City, we face each other at the dining table on twin computers and in the kitchen, one cooks while the other tackles clean up. But when my husband commands the steering wheel of an automobile, suddenly he thinks he can do without me.

"Turn right, honey," I plead, as we pass a landmark in rural New York State for the third time. "I think that's the way to the bridge," I say, wistfully pointing out the window as our car rumbles straight through the intersection. The crinkled map in my lap may offer no clue which gray squiggle represents this wooded country road, but I still think we should have turned right. Call it feminine instinct.

The man of my life is not listening. Nor is he watching the road. Instead, he's enamored with a new woman in the car. One hand on the wheel, the other is fondling a small Global Positioning System (GPS) unit mounted to the dashboard, the NeverLost Magellan.

Soon a breathy, female voice intones, "Calculating route. Make a legal U-turn."

My computer scientist husband swiftly complies, checking his mirrors as if the mechanized woman in the dash can appreciate his rigorous driving etiquette. Chafed, I realize he prefers feminine instinct packaged in a high-tech gadget worthy of James Bond.

"Approaching left turn in one mile," the disembodied lady voice continues. It's the turn I suggested, but now my husband is convinced. Our car has located the GPS satellites, computed our location and placed us on the grid. It's all very scientific. My man is bewitched by the small guidance screen highlighting our route in pink. When the car reaches the turn the machine makes the cloying sound of a 1950s doorbell.

Noticing my sour expression, he attempts to lighten my dark opinion of the device, enthusing over the instrument's slew of advantages: we can clock our time-to-destination, check our maneuver list, magnify the map. We can locate Chinese restaurants in the region

> Sometimes I wonder if men and women really suit each other. Perhaps they should live next door and just visit now and then.
>
> ◆
>
> —Katharine Hepburn

and view the next five exits. And then to add insult to injury, he points out that we can receive all this instruction in seven languages, including French, Dutch, Spanish and Japanese.

But, relieved of my navigating duties and with nothing else to do, I fume. Arms crossed, staring straight ahead, I think, "How galling to be sexy and precise in seven languages!" For all I care, she and my husband can both get lost. I am jealous of a travel gadget.

"Enjoy the sunset," he finally suggests, sighing, as we approach New York City, master-of-the-road saddled with a crotchety old mistress in the shotgun position.

Then tragedy strikes the happy new couple. Hoping to avoid thousands of vehicles entering Manhattan, my husband discovers he cannot suitably query the on-board guidance computer.

The James Bond woman is lacking in dimension and limits him to simple options: "Shortest Time," "Most Use of Freeways," and "Least Use of Freeways." The expensive little machine fails to factor the rush-hour time of night and the circuitous route we normally prefer to avoid the bottleneck.

Following the robotic navigator's strategy, soon we are mired in traffic near a bridge we wanted to bypass, and then end up in a tangle of New Jersey roadways before office buildings disrupt our signal and erase the on-screen map. My husband begins to lose his composure.

He's fidgeting with the machine and swearing, even though the device clearly states when rebooting that "Driver should not program while driving." This must be the first time he has defied the dame in the dash.

I'm smugly enjoying the dusk as instructed. We merge into an eight-lane highway heading west to California. An obvious mistake. Springing back to life, the computer offers a solution that seems easy but is impossible to execute among the dense traffic and poorly lit roads. Overloaded tractor trailers blast their horns as our car swerves uncertainly.

"What should I do?" finally my husband wonders aloud, jittery, inviting me to help devise a plan.

"Go south," I coach, eager to cooperate, willing to forgive. Keeping it simple. "We'll figure it out, sweetie." The metropolis of Manhattan looms, I am positive we can't miss it.

But the newly jilted bitch in the dash contradicts me, insisting in her firm and vaguely accented way, "Proceed to highlighted route!"

My husband, looking more like the man I married, reaches over and shuts off the misleading NeverLost. Seductive voice silenced, the screen goes dark. But as the city lights rise before us, I can still see the ghostly trace of her suggested itinerary.

A cultural essayist specializing in tales of personal adventure, Anastasia M. Ashman co-edited the nonfiction anthology Tales from the Expat Harem: Foreign Women in Modern Turkey. *Her writing on art, society, and culture has appeared in publications worldwide, from the* Asian Wall Street Journal *in Hong Kong to the* Village Voice *in New York. She currently lives in Istanbul with her Turkish husband, where she is at work on a travel memoir,* Berkeley to Byzantium: The Cultivation of a California Adventuress.

* * *

Mother and Child (and Disco) Reunion

There's nothing like a road trip for achieving
a kind of mushy enlightenment.

THIS IS YOUR BASIC GET-THE-HELL-OUT-OF-DODGE story. Like a kidney stone, I passed eight years of my life in Chicago. Love left me in '97 and had yet to find me in the two years that followed. Watching my ex date everything that moved and fall in love with the one who stayed still was not my idea of a "good time had by all"—all maybe except for me.

After several reconnoitering trips, the results were in:

1. San Francisco (too expensive, too snobby)
2. Boulder (too hairy)
3. Portland (too *Deliverance*)

I settle on Seattle. While I am no tree hugger, I like the idea of recycled plastic as outerwear, appreciate John Denver moments and already own four cloth grocery bags. Finding the preponderance of vintage VW buses "quaint," I sign a lease to live in Fremont (home of the Summer Solstice "bike naked" Parade). I then give notice in Wrigleyville where the closest I've been to naked lately is the sight of a pendulous beer gut swinging from a White Sox fan. The sick part is this memory will haunt me with a morbid fondness when I am far away from home.

Because I don't believe in shipping sentient creatures, I decide to drive myself and my dog, Disco, the 2,000 miles from Chicago to Seattle. I ask my mom to drive with us. Given the prospect of thirty-one hours in the car, I naturally assume my mom and I are on track for a real mother and child reunion, a basic remapping of the outer reaches of familial love, a supernatural bonding implosion. I figure my mom and I are going to make emotion worthy of a retrospective at The Whitney. I have visions of deep and meaningful conversations followed by that awe-struck floaty feeling I used to get when my sister and I had hyperventilating contests to see who could pass out first.

The morning of take-off, I bake a double batch of chocolate, chocolate-chip cookies, buy two super-size bags of turkey jerky, select my top

> ——)——
>
> People travel for myriad reasons. They travel because they crave adventure. They have dreams they've harbored for years that entail tropical beaches and too many margaritas. They want to walk among mystical castles and tragic ruins that harbor tales of passion lived long ago. They travel because they've always liked the idea of going somewhere different. They travel because they have two weeks of vacation and a desire to do something amazing with it. I started traveling because I got dumped.
>
> ◆
>
> —Jessica Erler,
> "Roman Womanhood"

twenty CDs including the '70s Preservationist Society, give Disco a doggie downer and head for O'Hare where I find my mom and her slim wheelie at Island 3 of the American terminal. I recognize her cotton candy poof of hair bobbing as she looks for me while standing semi-hidden behind the robust build of a fat-ass gentleman. The poof was how I used to track my mom down in the grocery store when I was little. After roaming around I'd walk each aisle looking above the shelf tops for the floating hair.

"Hi sweetie pie," my mom says giving me a hug, knowing this departure is a watershed event having arrived in Chicago a naïve twenty-six-year-old and now leaving bitter at thirty-four. Disco jumps up, paws on shoulder, to lick my mom and, like a sport, she sticks out her chin for some slobber. My mom is not a "pet person" but because she likes me, she likes Disco.

Within minutes we're all in the car, buckled up, the three of us gnawing jerky. "Look what I brought," my mom says handing me Eckard Tolle's *The Power of Now* on tape. Last year it was *The Art of Happiness*. I smile and toss the case on the back seat nailing Disco in the paw.

I hand all maps to the co-captain, put in some Joan Armatrading, hit the 90W and settle in for some hyperventilating conversation.

By Rockford, the dog has quietly vomited and my mom's asleep. Her head is conventionally thrown back, a cartoon lip pucker rhythmically sealing and unsealing like the opening to a balloon. She expels the softest "Pfooo." I begin counting, as you would to estimate the distance of lightning, "One one thousand, two one thousand…" Turns out my mom is 3.5 pfooo-miles away from me.

Driving alone gives me time to think:

- Why does "happy" rhyme with "crappy"?
- "Big-boned" means fat.
- Shit makes things grow.

This last thought strikes me as unusually brilliant. I say it out loud to see who's really sleeping and who's just pfooo'ing. Disco lifts his head as a nod to Master's brilliance then promptly nods off again, eye whites flickering forward and back—such commitment to being out of it. I look over at my mom to see how seriously asleep she is. Let's just say if human eyes could nictitate my mom would put the dog to shame.

Jerky bag #1 is empty which means I've consumed enough salt for a family of five…for a year. My not-so-local NPR station is fading as I cross into Minnesota, home of Garrison Keillor and his Prairie Home Companions. I give up on current events and, without compassion for the sleepy, fumble in the back for the bag of cookies which just so happens to wake the dog and mom.

"You were pfooo'ing," I say.

"Oh, was I?" she asks sipping some water. "Was I loud?"

Pfooo'ing loudly is a physical impossibility so I know she must still be sleepy. "Yeah, you woke the dog."

"I'm sorry Disco," my mom says turning around back to scratch his belly. "Oh, hey. Book time?" she asks. She eats a cookie and slides in cassette #1 of *The Power of Now.* "My friend Susan thinks Eckhart Tolle looks too much like a leprechaun to take anything he says seriously."

I take the cassette cover and quickly glance at the author photo. "No, just the opposite." I find this man so supernaturally fugly that he has just bought himself a lifetime supply of credibility. The last thing I need is a hottie telling me how to be.

Together, we zone out to the lullabic (not a word, but should be) tones of the English-accented reader:

To be identified with your mind is to be trapped in time: the compulsion to live almost exclusively through memory and anticipation. This creates an endless preoccupation with past and future and an unwillingness to honor and acknowledge the present moment and allow it to be. The compulsion arises because the past gives you an identity and the future holds the promise of salvation, of fulfillment in whatever form. Both are illusions.

I have my mom rewind this passage six times. Each time I focus on a different section and each time I banish the unenlightened thought I'll be meeting my husband naked on a bike.

By tape #2 neither of us can remember if we reversed when we should have flipped—nothing sounds familiar but nothing sounds quite new either.

"Are you waiting for a man or woman to give meaning to your life?" Eckhart, the homunculus, asks. I picture him perched just inside my frontal lobe clutching a four-leaf clover. My mom stares straight ahead and when I look at her she says, "No, not you."

> ──── ☽ ────
>
> M y mother always wanted a son-in-law, but I couldn't face calling her to tell her I'd be living in a one-horse Tunisian village as the wife of the police chief.
>
> ◆
>
> —Bonnie Mack, "Long Drive Through a Small Town"

By tape #4 I am so conscious of trying not to be used by my mind, to be in the now, that I feel like a Zenbot. I think about the miles whooshing past me and how they are sort of my *now* but just as quickly they are my *then* and I wonder if the tenets of the book should be modified for road tripping:

> Most people don't know how to listen because the major part of their attention is taken up by thinking.

Because I am only an aspiring Lilliputian I think:

- Who do I like better: Air Supply or ELO?
- Are there any circumstances under which I would consider a boob job?
- Why, if Jewish men and women are mixing their gene pools, do the women have rhythm and the men do not?

Feeling brilliant again I say this last one out loud. My mom, who is knitting now—a red, cashmere poncho with fringe—pauses a moment and then says, "I don't know."

I nod, knowing it's one of those unknowable things. I hold my hand out. "An extra chocolate-y one please." She reaches in the Hello Kitty bag and places a particularly lumpy cookie in my hand.

After a gas-and-pee-and-coke-slushy stop, my mom is driving now. Always open to new taste sensations, I dip a shard of jerky into my slushy and hand it to my mom. She tastes it and nods which means: don't do that again.

Fed up with now and the power of it, I put in a mixed CD self-titled, "All Covers All the Time" and crank up the Red Hot Chili Peppers doing "Brandy, You're a Fine Girl":

> "What a good wife you would be,
> but my life, my lover, my lady is the sea"

First of all, it's "are the sea" and second, "What a good wife you would be if only I could stop sailing my dick around the seven seas." As I say this out loud, my mom and

I look at each other—front teeth covered in chocolate—and throw our heads back and laugh.

Music is Disco's calling and to show he is a Jewish woman at heart he barks his head off and prances around in the back seat. I turn down the music. "It's O.K., Disco," my mom says scratching the sweet spot under his chin. He then calmly rests his head on my mom's left shoulder and closes his eyes as we barrel through the flatlands of Nebraska.

- What happens if you just have the kit and not the caboodle?
- No nagging feeling ever really goes away.
- Is Prince Matchabelli really a prince?
- What if Elvis sang "Oops, I did it again"?
- You're only as good as your worst photo.

We've traveled far, 1,500 miles, with an overnight in Bismarck, North Dakota during which Disco expertly performs the job no one gave him: to bark at all suspicious noises including his own farting. When he finally does sleep, it's on my mom's bed nestled up against her back. I feel betrayed, then pathetic, and finally, petty. It dawns on me I am in the middle of east bumble headed to pot-smoking, computer-geekville without a clue as to what I hope to do when I get there.

Eckhart Tolle's words drone on:

...the compulsion to live almost exclusively through memory...arises because the past gives you an identity and the future holds the promise of salvation... Both are illusions.

In my panic I start to cry. After a few moments of quiet crying, I kick it up a notch to get some attention. Disco notices first because, well, it's his job. Then my mom wakes up. I blow my nose.

"Are you O.K.?" she asks.

"Not really," I say.

"What's the matter?"

"Idon'tknowhatI'mdowhatthehellamIIdon'tIdon'tknoww hereI'mgoingandIandIandI…" and in the middle of all that I feel a nudge. It's my mom with her ticket (pillow) pushing me over as she crawls into bed beside me. She kisses my cheek, holds my hands and tells me it's going to be ok. Disco jumps up and paralyzes my left leg which is his way of saying, "Maybe, yes, maybe, no, but what are you going to do about it *now*?"

Epilogue: my mom liked the dog so much she got herself a cat.

Book author and humorist Laurie Frankel knows pain is the root of all comedy and is thrilled her life is so damn funny. When not penning grocery store haiku or telling it like it is, this former East Coaster can be found whooping it up in southern California. You can reach her at www.laurieslovelogic.com

ELIZABETH FONSECA

✳

The Ravioli Man

He had visions of dessert.

IF YOU ARE A YOUNG WOMAN TRAVELING ALONE, THERE
is one thing you can count on: lots of attention. Sometimes,
you might even want it.

On my first solo backpacking trip, I learned this truism.
It's the joy of solo travel: You meet many more people. It's
the bane of solo travel. You meet many more people.

I met the Ravioli Man through another guy I'll call
Hans, a curly-haired blond Swiss with sensuous lips whom I
met one day in the Tuileries. We got to walking, talking, I
was wary but curious. He looked striking in white, Good
Humoresque attire. My hotel, I said, was too expensive.
Turns out he knew a place. Still fool enough to listen to be-
guiling Swiss strangers, I packed my backpack, said *adieu* to
Laurent the desk clerk, and followed the ice-cream man to
another part of Paris.

Remember that it was summer, and there were few in-
expensive rooms at the inn. We emerged from the Metro
into a Dickensian scene of stump-legged beggars and belles

with brusque tones, ambiguous makeup, and rather less ambiguous track lines on their arms. But the room in the Hotel
Splendide was cheap and clean, and the tobacco-stained fingers of the night were encroaching, so I thought wistfully of
Laurent, said yes to the room and no to the ice-cream man
who, after much kissing and cajoling (his), went away.

I prided myself on my backpacker thriftiness, my con-
quest of a statuesque, limpid-eyed Swiss, my giddy placement
near the gritty underworld of the City of Light, and went in
search of libation. The bread-cheese-water combo was beginning to wear, doubly so by the certain knowledge of rich
creams and sauces stirred to silky smoothness behind the café
curtains of each brasserie—but I did have that Swiss Army
knife I had to keep in fighting trim. So I wended my way
back through the thickening cluster of ravaged women and
narrowly avoided baguette theft to arrive safely at my haven.

And that's when things got interesting.

No sooner had I laid out my repast on the tiny metal table
in my room than came a knock on my door. In my faulty
French and state of high suspicion, I asked who was there.
Lo, my concierge, concerned about the state of the water
supply in my room (I had a wee sink). Not yet the seasoned
traveler, I let him in. With an elaborate display of lingua
franca gestures and his and my broken French (he appearing
to be of Middle Eastern stock), I deduced that he felt the
trickle of water spilling from my faucet insufficient. It's nothing, I said, go away. He went. Exhausted from swatting away
amorous Swiss gents and lurid junkies, I was relieved.

I sat down to the chunk of cheese and was just then
breaking my crust of bread when I heard another knock.
Years of training demanded that I answer. It was my
concierge-cum-handyman, overly interested in the state of

my sink. Elaborate gestures, elaborate protests. Of course I had broken all the rules of logic and Hotel Splendide decorum by actually answering that knock, so the man sat on the rickety chair and eyed my dinner. Now he was concerned about my nutrition, and I about getting him and his roving eyes out, not to mention pondering how my discreet friend Laurent in the Hotel-Out-of-the-Backpacker's-Budget was doing right about then. After much operatic negotiation and repeated insistence that, no, I didn't want to share a meal with him, he went away.

Ah, peace! The cheese was pungent, the water a tonic, the bread perfectly crusty and my book a brace. I'd just shifted to a nice long stretch on the bed when—the knock again. It pains me to write this, but I answered. Only this time (the process of learning is slow and fraught with danger) I opened the door but a crack, blocking it with my shoulder in ready position to slam it shut. There was my concierge, a plate of steaming ravioli in his hand. He wanted to come in. Finally, I found the voice to be emphatic. No! I said, and slammed the door in his face. From the other side I heard, in a bewildered voice, this time in English, "But I am not Iranian!"

I went to sleep with my bed pulled in front of the flimsy door, wondering at the myriad implications of his one English phrase. I woke laughing, and just a short time later I kicked the dust of the Hotel Splendide off my shoes and shouldered my backpack, on to other adventures.

Elizabeth Fonseca has taught English in various locations around the world, including the Americas, Europe, and the Middle East. Her interests include travel, poetry, and cross-cultural communication. Overcoming her fear of ravioli, she has moved on to pen restaurant reviews and write for the Abu Dhabi Explorer *guidebook.*

COLLEEN FRIESEN

* * *

The Education
of a Guinea Pig

How do you say "My backside hurts" in Spanish?

IT'S KINDA HARD TO LOOK CASUAL WHEN YOU'RE PACKING a fluorescent orange Ziploc with a radioactive symbol on it labeled DANGER-BIOHAZARD-Specimen Bag. And how do you get rid of the bubblegum-purple medical gloves, the little cup and the wooden stool collection spoon when you're sharing a bathroom with a Guatemalan family and their only wastebasket has no lid?

It had all sounded so simple while I was safely at home and surfing the web. The banner proclaimed, "FREE SPAN-ISH LESSONS!!!" I just had to be a guinea pig in a Johns Hopkins University clinical trial for a vaccine against travel-ers diarrhea. I would merely agree to drink a slippery-salty concoction made up of killed E. coli bacteria and cholera. As long as I promised to check in with their nurses to provide blood, and "other" samples, they'd pay for three weeks of Spanish classes and a homestay in Antigua, Guatemala.

My less frugal friends (O.K., everyone I talked to) seemed incapable of recognizing the beauty of this offer. What's not to like? My twenty-year-old stepson was more astute than most. "Let me get this straight." He leaned forward for clarification. "They're *paying* you for your shit." Well yes, that's another way to put it.

Five A.M. I descend from the heavens into the bedlam of Guatemala City. I spot a taxi driver holding a battered piece of cardboard with a pretty close approximation of my name. I jump in his cab and am immediately wracked by doubt. I may be off the plane but now I'm really flying. Pedestrians are duly warned by blasting honks. Careening suddenly seems like such an evocative and completely right word. Riding shotgun also takes on a new meaning as we pass a Coca-Cola truck with an armed guard hanging from its side. There are bullet holes in the door panel. My taxi's cut-off seatbelts aren't doing much to reassure me. What is this some sort of cosmic test? Look God, no protection!

We turn off the highway and bounce along the cobbled roads down wall-lined *avenidas.* The taxi dives deeper into the maze of empty streets. How do I know it's me he's supposed to have in this cab? Where the hell are we? My mind is in that suspended frame I go to whenever I'm overwhelmed. I feel I have as much substance as a clay vase and about as many thoughts. Jesus just stares at me from his perch on the dash.

And then quite suddenly, my driver is gone and I'm alone in the cool dawn. The air is fragrant with the smell of damp stone. The guidebook warnings of muggings, thieves and murder are clamoring for attention in my feverish brain. I am standing in front of a crumbling wall facing the street that looks like every other crumbling wall facing the street. I buzz at various doors, hoping that the quivering jelly feeling in my belly is strictly from fear instead of the bacterial soup I drank last week. It already feels like forever ago but that's probably because it was on a different planet.

A battered wood door creaks open revealing a grinning woman. The little Spanish I know flies out of my head. All I remember is the not particularly useful phrase, "*Dos margaritas, por favor.* "Apparently, I've been on one too many all-inclusive holidays.

Vilma and Roberto are in their twenties with three children under the age of five. The entire family sleeps in one ten-by-ten room. This frees the two extra rooms for student rentals. The living room has nothing in it but a television and various pictures of a suffering Jesus and a much happier looking Mickey Mouse. The kitchen consists of a sink, one cupboard, stove, fridge, and blender. The table has five chairs. I am to sit with Anna, the other student. Every meal, while Vilma serves us, the family waits in their room either with Roberto or with their older cousin Rosa. We eat as fast as we can as we hear the children being shushed as they wait for their turn.

Vilma stands for hours at the large sink under the corrugated tin roof of her courtyard. She scrubs and rinses and wrings out diapers, shirts, little dresses and pants. In the evening she stands in the kitchen with a makeshift ironing board made of towels piled on the table. Each item emerges with crisp edges.

A couple times a week, I furtively head to the Johns Hopkins unit with my deposit. It's only a little cup in a baggie, although the baggie is festooned with that nuclear symbol, but my pack feels transparent. I can't wait to dump it in their little bar fridge with its magnificent poop magnet collection. I may not be able to conjugate all my *verbos* but I'm learning a new lingo. I tick off the box that says my stool was fully formed. An *episode* is described as "when the stool takes on the form of the cup." Sort of Dairy Queen style.

I'm delivering my goods and Johns Hopkins duly delivers theirs. Every day my free lessons help my struggling Spanish. I'm not quite ready for any discussions on existentialism, but I'm able to ask and mostly comprehend directions. So, on the weekends I board the chicken buses and head off to explore this world of light and shadow.

In the hotels I discover the same facilities that exist in my Monday to Friday home. That is, the *agua caliente* dial on the showerhead is more to inspire hope than actual hot water. Every day, proving the adage of hope springing eternal, I force the dial over to the hottest setting, trying not to touch the exposed wires. I then attempt to wash my hair without actually letting the cold trickle touch my head. I slime the wet around on my clammy skin, using the vile little pack towel that I promise to toss before I head home. I pull on my boring beige travel garb onto my damp skin. Khaki never looked so bland until I landed in a country where the women are dressed in direct competition with the parrots.

The last week of school my teacher Maria, who like me is female and in her forties, asks me to write about my typical day in Canada. I write that I like to have a hot bath every night. She stops me after that sentence.

"*¿Agua caliente?* Every night? You can lie down in water up to here?" She brushes back her blue-black glossy hair and holds her hand to her neck, her *café au lait* hand against the rainbow embroidery of her blouse.

"Do you like baths?" I ask, running my broken fingernails through my grubby hair. I am wishing desperately for *Jabon de San Simon.* The soap that promised to wash away my sins.

Unfortunately, it is at the bottom of my pack, useless against my current ignorance.

"I don't know. I've never had one...but it sounds very nice."

Colleen Friesen lives on the seaside in Sechelt, B.C. with her husband, their hyperactive twelve-year-old nephew, and a continuously shedding and occasionally incontinent Dalmatian named Mary-Margaret. Her work has appeared in A Woman's Asia, Whose Panties Are These?, *as well as a variety of magazines, newspapers, and websites.*

*

We entered a clearing that was all *ahhhh.* To our right, long narrow falls hurried over dark volcanic rock then thundered into a pool the shape of a half-moon. To our left, misty wisps floated over the hot springs that filled rocky crevices. Jungle-smothered cliffs gave way to sky blue.

Paradise's only fault? Other tourists. No problem, we'd wait them out. As the last French syllables were fading down the trail, we stripped and plunged into the pool. Billions of tingles shot through us as we dog-paddled towards the falls for a cold pummeling. Icy, we scrambled for the nearest steamy spring. Hot, cold, hot, cold: again and again, until all muscles were the consistency of an éclair's creamy insides. Then we collapsed neck deep each in our own bubbling crevice. Shadows lengthened. We reminded ourselves how fast dark follows sunset. We would agree it was time to go then sink back into our private pools and reveries. Strange noises entered my consciousness, so I rolled my head towards the trail, and...

Oh. My. Word. Dozens of soldiers were charging towards us. Black backs glistening as they ripped off their shirts. Black butts were next as shouting and calling to each other, they unzipped their pants. The man nearest me was buck naked—and laughing.

Guadeloupe's army advanced and not even the trusty "*au secours*" entered my head. My body leapt from torpor to torpedo in under ten seconds, streaking toward Karen and clothes. Adrenaline pumping, shirttails flying, and sneakers squishing we hurtled halfway down the trail. Then, bent over, hands on knees we gulped first for breath, giggles mounting to guffaws as it penetrated—we be big buffoons.

—Kate Crawford, "Uncovered in Guadeloupe"

* ✳ *

Keys to the Outback

They were hanging there the whole time.

"I CAN'T BELIEVE YOU LEFT THEM THERE," JIM MUTTERED as I squeezed the handle and pulled hard for a third time.

"What do you mean, you can't believe it? You can see them as well as I can. You're not going blind, are you?" The keys were clearly visible in the ignition. People were beginning to stare.

He walked around to my side of the car. "I knew this would happen if I let you drive."

"It has nothing to do with my driving." I circled to the passenger side to try that handle again. "My driving was fine. It's not as though you've never locked keys in the car." I wasn't entirely certain he ever had, but was willing to gamble on it to make my point. I wanted desperately to defend myself, because I suspected my mistake would have serious consequences.

We had rented our Holden wagon in Darwin, 300 miles away. At first, the man at the A1 Car Rental company tried to give us an old beater: no radio, one broken window, lots of dents, the whole thing covered in powdery red dust. "Yir goin' tuh Katherine? This's yir car, mate!"

The salesman looked at us incredulously when we complained. After some verbal wrangling, my husband, who is large and can be quite persuasive, managed to get us a late model station wagon with intact windows and a weak-but-functioning air conditioner.

Knowing we were in for long expanses of empty highway, we stopped at the edge of town to top off the fuel tank. "What's the speed limit, anyway?" Jim asked the attendant.

"What kin ya do, mate?"

"I said, 'What's the speed limit on the highway to Katherine?'" Jim repeated himself cheerfully. He meets strangers easily.

"What kin ya do?"

We hadn't anticipated any troubles communicating with the locals on our trip Down Under, but that had been naïve. Their accents were difficult to understand, the rhyming slang was impossible to decipher, and the wry Aussie sense of humor kept me off balance. I had become resigned to the fact that I was clueless much of the time, but Jim liked to maintain a sense of control.

About an hour out of Darwin we stopped to take each other's picture standing next to what the Aussies call "anthills." These aren't mere bumps of soft dirt, like American anthills. They are towering structures, sometimes as much as twenty feet high, built by termites out of their own saliva and feces. The resulting substance is so hard that the anthills were ground up and used instead of concrete to make airplane runways during World War II. Or so the Aussies said, and I believed them.

The instant we climbed out of the car, flies covered us both. Flies! Making themselves at home on my bare arms, crawling up my legs, doing their best to creep into my eyes and mouth. I tried desperately to shoo them away, but the flies were not deterred; they crawled over us with impunity. Billions of them live there—maybe trillions. I read that there are more than 650 separate species in Australia. The air was hot—easily 105 degrees Fahrenheit—and the land stretched out flat and dusty, with sparse vegetation and even fewer animals. I couldn't imagine how such a lifeless expanse could possibly support those buzzing hordes. What did they eat, anyway, when there were no tourists around?

We snapped our anthill photos fast and hopped back into the car. Hundreds of flies came with us. After some frantic experimentation, involving swatting, speeding, swerving, and swearing, we discovered that the best way to get rid of flies was to open all the windows and drive slowly. Of course this rendered the air conditioner useless, and we were soon dripping with perspiration, which caused the red Outback dust to cake onto our bodies in a most unattractive way. When I had exterminated all the flies but three, I climbed into the back seat and smashed the last survivors with our A1 rental papers. They left dry, brown smears across the part where we had signed up for extra insurance. Then we rolled up the windows and drove in silence, waiting for the car to cool off. It was too hot to talk.

As it turned out, there was, indeed, no official speed limit on the road to Katherine. Hundreds of miles of open road, dead straight, no Highway Patrol. The speed limit was whatever you could coax your car to do. I say "coax" because only a fool would take a high performance car on this road. When we stopped to get the camera, I discovered that the inside of the trunk was covered with fine red dust. The dust was also sucked into our luggage, and, inside that, into the plastic bag I use to protect the camera from dust. It gets into the engine, too, and the brakes. That was why the rental company had at first provided us with a beater for the trip. I began to feel guilty that we were ruining this A1 car for anything but Outback travel.

There were "speed limit" signs on the road: white rectangles with a big black zero in the center, and a slanted red bar crossing the zero. ("What kin ya do?") Jim took full advantage of this once-in-a-lifetime opportunity, and opened it up on the open road. When the speedometer hit 130 kilometers, I looked away. Mostly the trip was O.K., and even seemed fairly safe, because there were no other vehicles on the road. A couple of times we hit potholes and bounced hard. Once there was a really loud noise, and when I looked in the mirror I thought I saw something fall off the bottom of the car. But it was getting late, and we kept driving until we got to Katherine.

The next morning, the car seemed fine, and we took a dirt road out to Glen Helen, which is an outpost in the middle of nowhere. It consists of one gasoline pump, two camels in a small corral, a permanent looking "No Vacancy" sign, and a small motel-and-bar combination called the All Seasons Glen Helen Homestead.

There isn't much to do in Glen Helen, except to take a hike up the gorge, which is a dramatic contrast to the rest of the Outback. It was fun at first: a small stream gurgled along the trail, there were a few hardy plants, and the steep canyon walls sheltered us from the sun. Here and there a gray lizard skittered out of our path, but other than that, it was dead quiet. After a while we were too hot even in the shade, and we were tired and hungry, so we walked back to the roadhouse.

This is when we discovered I had locked the keys in the car. We had left our wallets safely in the glove compartment, since we wouldn't need them on the hike. (No need to carry any more than was necessary.) When we returned, we needed money to buy a couple of cold beers and some tucker (food). So there we were, circling the car, tugging the handles, arguing, hot and tired and hungry.

My clothes were sticking to my body. A fly landed on Jim's face, and walked into his nose. Until you have witnessed it, you cannot imagine how intensely irritable it makes a person when a fly crawls into his nostril and refuses to be dislodged.

It was at this point that we had the conversation about my driving.

Several helpful folks wandered over to view the keys dangling from the ignition and offer advice. "Why donja jus use yir spair key, mate?" one asked.

"This woonda happened if you'da left yir windars open," another offered.

The most practical of the lot suggested we simply throw a brick through the window, "She'll be right, mate!" When you're in the Outback, life seems fairly straightforward.

But there were no bricks to be had in Glen Helen, so I went inside, bummed some change, and phoned A1. It turned out the only spare key was in their Alice Springs office, more than eight hundred miles away. They said they'd send someone right over, as soon as they could round up an airplane. "No worries."

Waiting for the car keys to be delivered, Jim chatted up the waitress at the All Seasons Glen Helen Homestead—as I recall, he was not speaking to me at that time—and expressed his disgust over the hundreds of flies crawling on the outside of the window.

"Awwr that's nothin', mate!" she responded. "In the summa they completely cuvah ervery winda, so no light comes in uh'tall. Keeps the place coolah that way."

Hours passed. It was late afternoon, and I began to worry about where we would spend the night. There were no vacant rooms at the Homestead, and I was sure the Outback was at least as inhospitable at night as it was during the day. We couldn't even sleep in the car. There was no one to hitch a ride back to Katherine with; the travelers who were not staying the night had long since left. It was beginning to look like Jim might spend the night with the waitress, but what about me? I tried to remember whether Bedouins or other desert people slept with their camels, but could only dredge up stories of mean-spirited animals that spit and kick at humans.

I was in the middle of wondering whether lizards, which of course are cold-blooded, would be attracted to my body heat if I were sleeping in the desert, when a cheerful man in short shorts and an A1 shirt appeared and handed Jim the key, no worries. What did we owe him for this extravagant kindness? "Awwr, nothin' mate." He gave Jim a friendly slap on the back. "We'll sen'ja the bill laytah."

They did, too. Five months later a charge for sixty-five dollars showed up on my credit card bill. Sixty-five dollars— not even enough to pay for the airplane fuel! The description said simply, "A1 key delivery." Life is fairly straightforward in the Outback.

Laurie McAndish King has studied medicinal plants in the rainforests of Brazil and Argentina, chased lemurs through the mountains of Madagascar, fought off leeches in tropical Queensland, hunted a lion on foot in Botswana without a gun, and survived a kidnapping in Tunisia. Her Tunisian story, "At a Crossroads," was published in The Kindness of Strangers.

DEANNA SUKKAR

✳

Almost Grounded

This time they weren't groans of pleasure.

I MAKE MY WAY THROUGH THE PROVINCIAL LAOTIAN airport with the ease of an inveterate traveler. My backpack, festively covered with embroidered patches from such country delicacies as Cambodia, Swaziland, and Cuba, proudly salutes my exploratory spirit, if not my sewing prowess. I have been traveling for one month shy of a year. Walking by my side, with not quite the experienced swagger in her step, is my mom, carrying a baguette. She has decided to join me on the final leg of my global tramp.

The airport terminal boasts a corrugated metal roof, reed walls, and gravel floor. We check in and try to make ourselves comfortable for a long wait on chairs better used to stack canned goods. Looking about, I see deposited across from me three dazzling blue plastic bags. They are oddly rustling. Piqued, I sit up in my chair to scrutinize. Crammed inside, eyes bulging and throats pumping, are dozens of anxious frogs jumping randomly within their confines. Bemused, I pass several minutes watching before realizing that I am witnessing a break-out in progress—a determined handful seek liberty and are escaping their prison. This soon creates a mild ripple of excitement among the handful of Western tourists. A few mouths fall open mutely, followed by a smattering of whispers. One word eventually triumphs. "FROG!" This particular utterance dooms the fugitive riparians. The alerted amphibian merchant retrieves his slippery activists (none too soon in my book), and we all settle back down with contented sighs of amusement.

Ten minutes later, a man, thin as a chopstick and dressed tightly in uniform, approaches and in broken English informs me that there is a slight problem with my luggage. "Slight problem?" I ask. "Why yes, is ticking." My mother and I rejoin in a duet, "TICKING?!!" Ticking, in a piece of luggage, especially if it is emanating from *my* luggage, at an airport, does not sound "slight" to me. I am wholly perplexed. Did I let it "leave my sight?" One look at mom and I see that she has judiciously relegated her anxiety level about where to stay for the night, to second place. She looks around for suspicious characters, terrorist alert on orange. Best to nip *that* in the bud. I tell her not to worry. "Don't worry mom. I'll handle this."

I duly follow the guy down cement steps where some two dozen bags are awaiting their flight. As we descend, I reassuringly mumble to myself, "It can't be *my* bag ticking. I pack *so* light! I don't even use an *alarm clock*. Why do *I* have to investigate?" I am becoming increasingly indignant.

Three additional officials await my arrival; their cocked ears belie a contemplative calm. The bag in question is kind of balancing on top of the others, like a reclining Buddha. One of the young men indicates my closed pack with an uplift of his hairless chin. My cockiness gives way to curiosity. Looks like they haven't even opened it yet. I narrow the distance slowly. I am hearing a slight reverberation now, too…only, it's NOT "tick-tock." *Oh my God!* An overdue thought is entering my head, timidly surfacing at about the same speed as my hand is nearing my bag. My curiosity has fallen victim to unadulterated horror. I rest my palm on the surface and peek up at the expectant male faces. *Oh shiiiiiit!* The color of my face goes from white (shock) to green (sick) to red (wretched mortification), *and* back again, like an undulating Italian flag or a shimmering squid in the throes of courtship. What could they be *thinking*? How much English do they understand?

Feeling like one of those condemned frogs awaiting a sautéed garlic finish, and yearning for home (or spontaneous ascension), I unzip leisurely, playing for time, composure, and air. Out of my plastic toiletry bag, I extract my three-inch, mercifully non-descript, éclair-shaped vibrator. Regrettably, it has been blithely working overtime and is humming tirelessly, its own private party.

How I wish at this moment that it had missed my "packing light" cut a year ago. In retrospect, I must have confused necessity with luxury. I mean, how lazy can a woman be? Ben Franklin firmly avowed, "Sloth makes all things difficult, but industry, all things easy." Nay, he was indeed *not* speaking of such an electric frivolity. Nevertheless, over two centuries later, I have proven him correct. Couldn't I have seen fit to be a bit more "industrious?"

The first thing I do, after turning off the little traitor, is smile innocently at the poker faces, dismissively shaking my head. Then I resort to what any loyal daughter would do. I blame it on my mom. "I am *sooooo* sorry. Heh, heh, I guess my mother's massager has gone off. On. Sore shoulders you know. She's not used to lugging a pack." To prove my point, I deftly apply it to my left deltoid, squint my eyes, and emit an *aaaaaah*. The men are grouped together like a nascent banyan tree, staring at the culprit with a collectively raised eyebrow. Is third from left smirking? *Humph*. Apart from my neon face, *I* think I am handling this with aplomb, commendably trying to spare our little group gratuitous embarrassment. I nimbly pop the device back into the little sack, next to my earplugs. Grinning sheepishly, I make a calculated point of storing the batteries separately. The four musketeers are exhibiting a stealth approximating that of my chocoholic sister guarding a diminishing cache of chocolate. Seeing this temporary cessation of activity, I speedily offer up a few more apologies, turn around with deliberation, and start walking away, knowing that all eyes are fastened on *me* now. At the foot of the stairs I turn, do some sort of bowing thank-you thing, and with a pathetic wave, flee. No one follows.

To this day, I wonder what was going through the minds of those silent comrades. Did I really fool them? Or is this a story that veteran airport employees in Laos share with incoming trainees? And then there's mom. To spare myself further humiliation, I never told her the truth that day. In fact, I am sure she hasn't given the incident a second thought…until now.

Deanna Sukkar is a lapsed professional chef who has taken off her toque blanche and set down her knife. Pursuing her Master's Degree in Library and Information Science at the University of Washington, she now slings a backpack full of textbooks. Her first story appeared in Whose Panties Are These? *She still scratches her travel itch, but the only battery-operated device she packs now is her camera.*

✳

This year I will be traveling by airplane at the height of flu season, just before Christmas. I'm finding myself with a fear of flying for another reason. I haven't had a flu shot.

We can hardly weed out potential flu spreaders like we weed out potential terrorists, plucking a runny-nosed woman out of line and ejecting her to the airport doctor for further questioning. But the thought of sharing recycled airplane air for five hours with hacked-up potential flu germs scares me silly.

If only there were a way to quell the spread of germs by inconsiderate sick people who cough, cough, cough, without covering their mouths in tight corners such as an airplane.

How about fines? Yes, implement a $100 fine for each cough, $500 for each sneeze. People would think twice then before letting loose a string of germ-riddled snot and saliva. And, if we're going to go this far, why not impose a $20 fart fine? Just for the sake of good manners.

—Jennifer Brown, "Fear of Flying"

ELIZABETH ASDORIAN

* * *

The Naked
and the Wed

They all enjoyed a divorce from their clothes.

"WATCH OUT FOR THE NUDIES, MON," ADVISED VALENTINE, the bartender we had affectionately named "most stoned at work." It was a toss-up between him and the extremely buzzed Charlton, but when we caught Valentine desperately shoving maraschino cherries—stems and all—in his mouth when he thought no one was looking, we knew we had our winner.

"No one want to be out there pouring them drinks. They be crazy, mon." Scott and I were getting the finer points on enjoying our stay at the couples-only Jamaican resort we had been lured to by the promise of unlimited cocktails and utter relaxation. It was not exactly our style, but we were actually enjoying ourselves in a "watching people at the airport" sort of way. Plus, we were really, really drunk.

"So it's clothing optional?" I asked Valentine, of the small island offshore that was one of the resort's main selling points in our book. In my not-a-fan-of-weird-tan-lines opinion, if you're going to cook your skin in the tropical sun, why not broil the pasty nether regions as well?

"No option, mon. No clothes period. It's the rule." Valentine tried to nod forcefully, for effect, but it looked more like he was losing consciousness and fighting to keep his head from falling into the blender of "Hummingbirds" he was making for an inebriated couple to our right.

"You have to be *naked* the whole time?" asked the woman, with a disgusted tone, as if she'd spent her entire life fully clothed and had only heard rumors about what was under *there*.

"Yah, from the time you get off the boat, off come the clothes, mon. And you know," he paused, as if he was making one of those truly profound discoveries that only really stoned people make, "sometimes clothes are good."

Valentine had a point. But we were still intrigued by the island. We would definitely pay it a visit. As soon as we slept off our incredible hangovers.

The idea of mandatory nakedness burrowed into my brain as I watched a couple I hoped I would never see naked walking down the aisle the next morning. It was not just another twenty-four-hours in paradise, it was Valentine's Day, the worst possible day any two grumpy, jaded people could arrive at a resort for "lovebirds." It was the official, Hallmark card-sanctioned holiday that made people everywhere feel desperate to be in love or prove they were in love. No good could ever come of Valentine's Day, in my book. And the sixteen weddings scheduled at the beach gazebo before noon were vivid proof.

The groom in question was marrying a much younger woman, although they seemed equals in the saggy skin department. Their journey down the path was wobbly and uncertain, hinting at too many breakfast Hummingbirds or perhaps the realization that they were getting hitched thou-sands of miles from home, and life might not feel so footloose and beachy when they got back to Toledo. "Have they seen each other naked?" I wondered. "Am I going to bump into them and their naughty bits on that damn island?"

It became a phobia for the rest of the day. Every new husband, every new wife, every new wedding party filled me with prickly dread.

What was the proper etiquette for congratulat-ing the freshly betrothed when they were both without clothes? "That was a beautiful dress you were wearing earlier—*you should have kept it on.*" "I can tell you two love each other a lot—*it says so right on your tattooed butt.*" Or, "Like I always say, nothing spices up a marriage like nipple rings!" Miss Manners would have had just the perfect pleasantry, but I was at a loss.

I kept trying to dissect my fears—why was I so afraid of seeing these newlyweds out of their wedding finery and in their birthday suits? I've spent lots of time at nude beaches.

> ─── ☽ ───
>
> From sandaled teens in spandex shorts to dusty crones in shapeless dresses, the women of Bucharest exhib-ited a certain freedom. Nipple shadows smudged thin, sum-mer fabrics. Breasts bounced and jiggled. I was the only woman on Independence Boulevard wearing a bra. My inch of cleavage, daring on the airplane, now seemed dull. My bra felt like armor, chain mail at the feast after the battle is won.
>
> ◆
>
> —Carol Stigger,
> "Braless in Bucharest"

I'm no prude. So why was the thought of running into a recently Mr. and Mrs. out there causing such angst?

Despite my fears—or maybe because of them—Scott and
I just couldn't tear ourselves away from the procession of
processionals and head out to the island. Instead, we collected
an assortment of boozy beverages, planted ourselves in a cozy
tree swing by the peeing cupid fountain, and spent a morning watching the sanctity happen.

We saw a group of groomsmen dressed, inexplicably, like
park rangers, posing for warm, loving photos before a wedding. Would they be stripping off those brown short sets after
the ceremony and frolicking just as playfully?

We saw a woman, unbearably sunburned, her slinky dress
revealing the sad consequences of her sunscreenless yesterday.
Luckily, she would most likely be in a tub of medicated aloe
this afternoon.

We saw a groom mug for the camera and do the "respect"
hand smash with the videographer. Crap, that show-off
would definitely be out there on naked island.

Love, Caribbean-style, was in full bloom. And we dutifully
witnessed sixteen, fifteen-minute ceremonies—four hours of
non-stop "romance"—that would have disheartened even
Eros himself.

"I've never see so much red and white in my life," Scott
said of the balloons, streamers, crepe paper, floral arrangements, napkins, forks, spoons, and now, garbage, that was
strewn all over the gazebo.

"Just think how much red and white we'll see out there,"
I replied, nodding my head towards the island. "You know, all
that newly married *skin*."

And in the warm Jamaican sun, I swear we both shivered.

We returned to the bar for more free cocktails. Valentine

was there, picking at a banana. He looked extremely stoned, but grumpy.

"I hate this day," he confided, as we sat down in front of him.

"Yeah, you must have heard the "Valentine" thing a million times today," I said, sympathetically. Drunken people do have a habit of stating the obvious. "We hate it, too. It's so contrived."

"No mon. It's that," he said and pointed to a trashcan filled with the remains of sixteen tiny, red-and-white wedding cakes. "They make all them cakes today and people be wasting them." He sighed and took a small bite from the fruit, obviously unsatisfied with the low sugar content of his munchie selection. Poor Valentine. There were at least ten more weddings—and ten more coveted, unattainable pastries—he'd have to deal with for the rest of the day.

We, however, were done with wedding watching. And as the sun peaked in the sky, it was time. We were juiced up on coconut rum and ready to get sun-baked ourselves. So we hailed the small boat to take us to the island.

After no more than three minutes we were there. I felt my throat constrict, just a little. As the boat pulled to shore, the driver looked at us expectantly. "Does he want a tip?" I wondered. No, tipping wasn't allowed at the resort. That couldn't be it. He continued to stare and I realized: *he's waiting for us to take off our clothes.*

The pressure was a little too intense, so we kept our cover-ups on for the short walk up the rocks to the center of the island action. There was a festive beachside bar. Tropical drinks. Lounge chairs. Umbrellas. And about thirty naked, tipsy people crammed into a hot tub.

They stopped mid-conversation and gawked at us, the only people other than the poor, beleaguered bartender wearing anything besides tattoos and body piercings. I took a quick peek—at just the faces, of course—and saw no one familiar from the wedding marathon of the morning. Relief washed over me like a bottle of warm sunscreen. I smiled and waved at the mass of arms, legs, and whatnot pruning in the water.

Fears allayed, Scott and I stripped down and enjoyed feeling the sunshine where, normally, the sun doesn't shine.

I was ready for another cocktail, so I walked to the bar and ordered a Rum Runner from the necessarily shifty-eyed waiter. And as I turned back towards our chairs, there she was.

The sunburned bride from today was braving blisters and most likely a hellacious case of melanoma to be out here on the naked island with her new husband. They smiled politely as I moved towards them, and my brain went into overdrive, thinking of something to say.

"Saw you today, well, less than I'm seeing you now, but, you know." No, that wouldn't work. "Great wedding." That sounded really sarcastic. "How's it hanging?" No, that was just juvenile.

"Hello," they said.

"Hello," I replied.

And that was it.

I went back, lay down, and tried to analyze what had just happened. Why was I completely indifferent to a tub full of nude sunbathers, but one just-married couple totally weirded me out?

Finally it dawned on me. It wasn't about nudity; it was about exposing too much. They weren't just showing their bodies—and all the many, many, many flaws associated with them. They had exposed something even more naked about themselves today. Their romantic hopes. Their dreams of finding "the one." Their basic human need and desire for love.

The fact that they were here in Jamaica on the Superbowl Sunday of romance getting married showed they weren't jaded or sarcastic or believers in the harsh statistics that said they would most likely be divorced within three years. These were optimists—naked optimists. They wore their hearts on their sleeves, without even needing a shirt.

I realized I wasn't afraid of seeing "nudie-weds" without clothes; I was afraid of seeing them without pretense.

As if on cue, the first married couple of the day arrived on the boat. They gleefully disembarked and disrobed, flashing themselves for the all the world to see. But as I watched them laugh and kiss, I didn't see buttocks or breasts or even, horrors, "twigs and berries."

I saw two people in love on Valentine's Day.

Elizabeth Asdorian is a freelance copywriter whose advertising work has appeared in Print, Creativity *and* Archive. *Her foray into travel writing, "Midmorning Express," is included in* Whose Panties Are These? *and* Italy, A Love Story. *She lives with her husband and daughter in San Francisco where she occasionally runs into naked people, but can't be sure if they're newlyweds.*

AMY C. BALFOUR

* ✳ *

Just Another Malibu Minnie

The author makes a fashion statement at her first triathlon.

IT WAS COLD. IT WAS DARK. AND SOMEWHERE BETWEEN my car and the port-o-john line, I'd determined I was the Barney Fife of triathletes. The nerd of the herd. Goofy, inept, and continually surprised by the obvious. As I looked at my fellow racers on this cold, dark morning, the morning of my first triathlon, it was becoming obvious that one of these things was not like the others, and that thing just happened to be me.

I should have been psyched. I'd been asked to join a relay team called the Three Minnies. We were racing with the Disney Tri-Club in the Nautica Malibu Triathlon, and I was riding the bike leg on the most scenic road in America. An eighteen-mile excursion along the Pacific Coast Highway from the white sands of Zuma Beach to the coastal flowers of Carrillo State Park and back again. The other two Minnies, Kiran and Rory, had lured me to the competition with whispers of celebrities, food, and hunky bikers. "And it's for charity," they added. "It'll be fun." Who was I to resist the sirens' call? I pictured myself a stylish Malibu Minnie, nibbling cheddar cubes and flirting with sexy Mickeys after an invigorating ride. And it was for charity to boot. Flirting and feeling good about myself all at the same time. What more could a single Minnie want?

But cheddar dreams turned to Velveeta nightmares while waiting in line for a port-o-john, a wait just long enough to allow me to observe the competition and reach a depressing pre-race conclusion: "I'm totally out of my league."

First clue? My outfit. While the kind-hearted might've called my white cotton t-shirt "old school," in reality the only message it proclaimed was "nerd school." A point hammered home as the sun rose over the gray port-o-potties, and I saw the shirts of my competitors. Stretchy synthetic tops that clung tightly to ripped abs. Shirts with more functionality than most of my friends. Shirts that could "wick," shirts that could "breathe." Give them a year, and these shirts would be whipping up lobster bisques and crème brulees while their owners took post-race showers.

And the colors, I thought, as I finally stepped into a portable gray toilet. Flashing purples. Dashing reds. These shirts were fast. These shirts were moving ten miles an hour standing still. But not my cotton t-shirt. It was white. It retained water. It clung to my body like a fried egg on a wet burrito. The only thing my shirt had going for it was the fact that it covered my ass. And ah, my ass. It looked twice its normal size because of my padded tights. Now padded tights aren't bad in and of themselves. Most bikers wear them to avoid sore butts on long rides. But padded tights gave their butts a little more personality. Just enough personality to be considered cute. But I'd moved past cute into whole new dimension—a dimension begging to be covered by a pair of lavender bike shorts. Shorts so heinous, so purple, that they screamed to the passing masses that I was, indeed, a pear. A pear in a bowl full of power bars. A pear that was about to get bruised.

"Hey you! Need a number?"

I looked right. A perky surf chick smiled, waved a magic marker at me. "C'mon, dude, beat the crowd," she said. Beat the crowd? For what? Free stuff? Count me in, I thought as I wandered over. "What's your event?" she asked.

"Women's relay," I responded, looking for my free gift.

"Age?" asked the Surf Chick, all smiles as she crouched by my leg, marker poised above her head like a spear.

"Thirty-seven?" I replied as her marker zoomed onto my calf.

"Ooops," she murmured.

Ooops? What's ooops? Me no like the sound of ooops, Surf Chick. I looked down to see *Relay* scrawled across my leg in black. Underneath was a giant 37. Surf Chick had written my age on my leg in black ink! Well, sort of. I leaned closer. Surf Chick was no Michelangelo. The seven was a big scratchy blob that could also be a nine. That's a key two years to a single gal, my dear. How do I pick up a celebrity with a big 39 on my leg? Maybe I'll wash it off and start over. Twenty-eight was a good year. I'll create a new identity. No last name. No back story. Just 28. I'll start fresh....

"Amy, come on! We need to get going," yelled Kiran. I looked up, smiled, waved, and realized why Kiran was ready to get going. She had a 31 on her leg. Things are good when you're 31. Not so good when you're 37. Or 39. Maybe I should grab the marker. Add that I like long walks on the beach. A 37 looking for a 38 to 42. Single. Own bike. Likes celebrities. Queen of the Nerds.

I followed Kiran to the staging area where my nerdiness went from bad to worse in 3.2 seconds. Rory, seeing me approach in my white cotton t-shirt and lavender shorts, stopped adjusting her wetsuit. She grimaced, obviously displeased with my "look." She took a breath, smiled, and reached deep into her knapsack.

"Wear this," she whispered, giving me a sympathetic pat on the shoulder as she passed me a shirt. As she trotted off toward the beach, I took a closer look. It was a Disney Tri-Club racing jersey—a yellow Lycra shirt with black Mickey Mouse ears emblazoned on the front. I slipped it on. Too bright. Too tight. I am nerd, hear me squeak.

For the next twenty minutes or so I paced, checked my bike, planned my escape. But before I could go AWOL, the first male swimmers were emerging from the sea. After rounding a corner at the north end of the Zuma Beach parking lot, they ran south toward the transition area, looking to tag their biker for the next leg of the race. I watched the transitions with awe. These guys were so fast, so smooth, that for a moment I forgot my inner nerd.

"You might want to get ready," Kiran said, breaking the spell.

What? Get ready? Rory has to swim half a mile for Pete's sake, and the men are still coming in. I've got time girlfriend, relax.

"Oh my God! There she is! Get your bike!" Kiran yelled.

What? I looked up. Rory was indeed dashing toward us. Or me rather. Had it even been half an hour? Had she done so well she was running with the men? Shit! I yanked my bike from the rack, maneuvered it through a cheering maze of yellow-shirted Disney racers.

"Go Amy, go!" Kiran yelled, pulling me forward for the transition. And whatever you think you know about the word graceful? Picture the exact opposite and you'll have some understanding of my scramble toward the gate.

I pushed though a sea of triathletes, running beside my bike. At the gate, I hopped on without falling and rolled forward, the crowd going wild at the sight of a woman starting the bike leg. Too bad that woman was me. Me in my tight yellow jersey and huge purple pants. Please don't take my picture! I'm an imposter! I don't know what the hell I'm doing! All I know is my jersey's creeping up my stomach and soon you'll be cheering my breasts! Or laughing. Look away, people, look away.

I pedaled south out of the Zuma Beach parking lot, pumping like my life depended on it as I tried to maintain Rory's lead. As I swung onto the Pacific Coast Highway, I started a slow climb up a long, tough hill.

"Good work Disney!"

I looked left. A yellow-shirted Disney biker was speeding past.

"Thank you," I gasped.

"Keep it up Disney," yelled another, passing seconds later.

"Thank you!" I yelled.

"Go Disney!" said another.

"Thank you," I replied.

"Good work Disney!"

"Thankyouthankyouthankyou," I gasped again. And again. And again. Was I being passed by every member of the Disney Tri-Club, not to mention the other 1,500 or so registered bikers? What was the etiquette here, I wondered. Was it rude not to thank them? Maybe I should save my wind. Maybe I should just nod. Or maybe yell "Go Disney!" in return. Maybe I'm an idiot. Maybe I should've clarified this with Kiran and Rory. Maybe I should stop stressing and pedal.

After an eternity of pedaling and gasping, my purple-padded ass and I made it to the top of the first hill. On my descent, I decided to appreciate this new experience. The new sights. The new smells. This was the most scenic part of Malibu after all, and it was nice to enjoy it outside the confines of a car. The blue Pacific rippled calmly on my left, lazy mountains rolled gently on my right. Life was good, I wasn't last, it wasn't raining, and…

"There's no coasting on Team Disney!"

I looked left, swerving out of my reverie. The General George F. Patton of cyclists snarled as he powered past, disdain wicking from his bright yellow jersey.

"Aye, aye, General! Disney don't coast!" I thought, snapping to attention and pressing down on the pedals.

After another sixteen miles and forty-two additional "Go Disneys!" I rolled into the Zuma Beach staging area. I hopped off my bike at the gate, wobbling as I hurried toward Kiran for the transition to her four-mile run. After tagging off, I gasped one last "Go Disney!" before collapsing in a heap on the black concrete. And there I lay, exhausted and panting, hoping someone would carry my thirty-seven-year-old prostrate body to the celebrity tent. Cheddar cubes, celebrities, and free smoothies.

After waiting ten minutes with no relief in sight, the obvious became apparent. If I wanted to enjoy the celebrity tent, I'd have to drag my nerdy ass over there myself. I took a breath, stood, and dragged my rusty, nerdy bike to the bike rack. I dusted myself off and headed toward the tent, sweaty, tired, and a just a little proud in my tight yellow jersey and padded purple shorts. As Lance Armstrong so famously wrote, "It's not about the bike." Of course not. It was about Sheryl Crow. Celebrities. Glitterati. The good life. So get out of my way. If this was a celebrity-studded event, I wanted my celebrity stud.

So I entered the big, white tent, bold and invigorated, just daring someone to ask me to leave. But it appeared I was in luck. The Queen of the Nerds had raised enough in pledges to ensure admittance without question. I looked around, taking a long breath as I scoped out the food. The drinks. The celebrities.

"Weren't you on *Survivor?*"

I turned at the question. Behind me, a gangly triathlete was standing beside a bearded young hunk. Awkward, sweaty, slightly delusional, the triathlete gazed at the C-list star—a twenty-something hunk who'd been voted off Mark Burnett's island at some point in the recent past.

The young hunk nodded, smiling at the recognition.

"Wow, I watched every one of your episodes," the triathlete said. "And I just want to tell you, I thought you did a great job. I really admire your work."

And with that cheesy line, the torch was passed. The crown of dorkdom had been lifted from my head and placed on another. The queen is dead, long live the king. This Malibu Minnie was free.

Amy Balfour practiced law in Richmond, Virginia before moving to Los Angeles to break in as a screenwriter. She's a writer's assistant on Law & Order: Special Victim's Unit *where she writes Fed Ex labels and phone messages, simultaneously hoping to be noticed and ignored. She's hiked to the bottom of the Grand Canyon, rafted the Gauley River during dam release, and run with the chickens in Collierstown, Virginia.*

MELINDA MISURACA

. * .

Blinded by Science

When the universe calls you,
you come.

ABOUT AN HOUR OUT ON THE LONGTAIL BOAT TO
Phranang, I feel the stabbing reminder of those six cups of
tea. They'd gone down in a teahouse in the seaside town of
Krabi, while I was chatted up by a Thai love prince who
had emerged in the center of my karmic field. With a ritual
softness he poured cup after cup of jasmine tea, while from
his lips tumbled strings of monosyllables, pearls he'd gleaned
of my language. *You, me, go.* I wanted to respond in kind—
what more needed to be said?—but I was quiet. He
watched me for signs of melting, his eyes watering with
such a tragic thirst that I suffered chest pains when I heard
the boatman's call. He was a man, and I was in recovery
from just such an affliction. I departed forever from the idea
of him, the bursting forth of its many possibilities. I'm sure
you can understand how easily one could forget, wavering
between impulse and intention, to attend to one's physio-
logical details.

The boat is slim, curlicued at the end like the proboscis of an exotic insect. There are about twenty of us in various stages of heat-induced delirium, traveling on Thailand's Andaman Sea. About half are foreigners, there for the dubiously pure experience—to my left is a big blonde with a German flag sewn to her backpack and an alarming tropical disease on her leg. When I squirm away from her on the narrow plank seat, the boat rocks to and fro, provoking scowls from the tourists and smiles from the Thais.

I consult my English-Thai pocket dictionary. *Law diou,* I say to the boatman, attempting an elegant diphthong. I gesture to the shore. He looks through me like a window. My condition is not yet desperate enough for a pantomime, so I distract myself by following the movements of an elderly Thai lady seated to my right, cool and content in the generous shadow of her lampshade hat. I watch as she takes out a wooden box, removes several ingredients—a green leaf, a white nut, some black paste—bundles them together and stuffs the whole package in her mouth. In seconds she has it chewed down to a manageable wad.

The lady feels me watching. She projects a gob of blood-red saliva that shoots six feet past the side of the boat, turns and motions that I ought to try some. I politely decline in that nodding way I've seen Thais do. I'd read that betel nut chewing is a respectable pastime of older Thai women, yet don't think I've quite come of age.

First lesson learned in Thailand: Be ye not well-hydrated on a lollygagging longboat. The gentle lapping of the river against the boat's hull is as dangerously hypnotic as a self-help CD: *Relax, let go,* it whispers. *Allow every part of your body to become heavy, verrry heaavy, releasing anything you are holding on to.*

I do not relax. I double-cross my legs, recruiting about twelve different muscles in a team effort to barricade my bladder. How I will later stand and exit the boat is a bridge I will slosh across when the time comes.

We near the Phranang shore. Only later am I fully able to appreciate the massive rock formations jutting out of the water, like giant elephants lumbering across the sea. Right now I have my eyes locked upon a little structure next to the pier. I can just make out two letters painted on its door: WC. I stare at it as if it were a sacred mandala.

I am the Buddha under the Bodhi tree, as Immovable as a Mountain.

The Thai lady takes a tea kettle out of a basket.

I am a Fortress, a Locked Trunk buried in the earth.

She pours some tea into a glass—

I am a Frigid Housewife, a Dead Whale.

—and holds it out to me.

Dang.

I dare not shake even just my head. I have reached a pinnacle upon which I teeter, a dilemma that has followed me throughout my life: I must choose to either keep my dignity or cut the ties that bind me, between the discipline of holding back forever and the flagrant flinging open of the gates to freedom.

I waver. I try not to wobble. I hold on for a life-altering moment while mumbling something to the German girl about keeping a eye on my stuff. I can't hear her response because I am diving into the sea, relief spreading through my body before I even hit the water.

When I surface, I have been born again under a lucky star. I swim, victorious, toward the fabled white sands of Phranang, just another American fool, slogging out of the water and over to where my new German friend waits, pissed off, with my pack. "*Danke schön*," I say, as she stomps away. I decide to sit on the beach and dry off a bit before I look for the night's bungalow. As I watch the stars sidle out, one by one, I feel as though I have just untied a heavy anchor that had weighed me down forever. Vast populations are fluttering in my bloodstream: dragonflies and butterflies and golden honeybees of love. The nerve endings on my skin spring to attention, exuding pheromones from every pore. The me of yore—the harlot, the trollop—would have planned ahead, would have snatched up that yummy little treat back at the teahouse with whom to indulge in my randy persuasion. Alas! I am as unaccompanied as a clam.

I'm watching the waves, and the sparkles inside me appear to be floating there as well, as if a galaxy of heavenly bodies had been flung across the sea. Then, a humanoid form rises up from the water, glowing from head-to-toe. I frantically pat myself for outgrowths of dementia. Is that a narcotic rush I'm feeling? Maybe, back in Krabi, some upcountry opium had been sprinkled in my tea! The last time I'd tripped was during a peyote ritual gone awry, the one that had manifested a ten-thousand-fold hallucination of my high school algebra teacher, Sister Ursula. She'd sprouted Hinduesque undulating arms, her millions of chubby hands each grasping chalk, and a great omnipresent mouth that bespoke: *There are Vastly Compelling Reasons to find the Roots of Unity.*

The sparkle-clad figure is heading my way. I leap to my feet and run like the dickens, an instinct that has served me well when I've listened to it. I run along the beach, toward a tall, rocky outcropping. I find a cave. The fragrance of incense and a soft, flickering light beckon me into its recesses.

Dang!

Scores of wooden penises—in a multi-culti rainbow of colors and dimensions—are wedged, stacked, glued with melted wax to the surface of a candle-lit altar. These are the most alert save-the-race likenesses I've ever seen, their angles of repose ranging between 45 and 90 degrees—a sort of *Kama Sutra* lesson in geometry. Some are decorated with squiggly Thai script. Others are rather banged up, evidence of past abuse. I spy a contingent of thumb-sized red guys with black helmet heads, all lined up in military formation, a forearm-sized member presiding over them. Meanwhile, humongous phallic shadows waltz across the walls of the cave. Something inside me churns.

"Penises," I bellow, as if the word could open a magic door.

"Pardon me?" a deep voice answers behind me.

I jump. It's a man. A Brit, by the sound of him. He's dripping, must've just come from an evening swim. He wears the teeniest, tightest cutoffs I've ever seen on a man. Ignoring this unnerving stylistic detail—*Is it a Euro thing?* I wonder—I notice his hazel eyes and dark, well-groomed beard. He smiles and holds out his hand.

"I'm Noland," he says. "I saw you running, figured you were another Yank who'd fallen off her trolley. Or perhaps you've come to place an offering on the altar?"

"Melinda," I say, and shake his hand. It is warm, wet. "I'm afraid I don't have a, um, phallus with me. Do you have one I could use?"

Noland laughs. "The Thais call this the Princess Cave," he says. "The local fishermen pile these little beauties in here to honor the sea goddess, hoping for good fortune at sea. And in the bedroom, of course. Thai legend has it that she gave birth to a man, whom she created to be her lover. He would come down to the water to meet her and they would frolic in the waves."

I shiver. "I could've sworn I saw somebody, *glowing,* in the water…"

"'Twas I!" Noland says. "Covered in phosphorescent plankton. Dinoflagelletes, specifically, with flagellating tails."

"Flagellating tails?"

"Like sperm," he says, rubbing a thumb and forefinger together in a circular motion. "A bit slimy, yet kind of tacky."

He's looking at me intently.

"The dinoflagellates, I mean," he says, reddening.

We talk some more. Noland tells me he is an anthropologist, taking a break from field work in Malaysia. Came to Phranang to do some writing.

"About life in the bush?" I ask.

"Poetry," he says. "Letting all the smells and tastes and everything I've absorbed for the last eight months float up to the surface, burst out of me and onto the paper."

"I know what you mean," I say. "I think some of those dino-flago numbers got into the drinking water. I've been sending home cryptic postcards about being brainwashed by squids, buddhas, and Thai beach boys."

"Lovely!" says Noland.

And he is. Lovely. Especially lit by candles and surrounded by penises, which I stare at to avoid flagellating into his eyes. My heart is throbbing as ecstatically as a rave dancer, replicating itself in all the errant places of my body that I've been trying to ignore for the last several weeks. That little emergency vial of rationale I keep on the top shelf of my mind, the one that comes complete with a subliminal tape-loop of my shrink's voice, which to listen to is equivalent to wearing a chastity belt—I feel it explode from the high-voltage current coursing through me.

As my last few shreds of decency and restraint take flight,

I have an idea: A compilation of phallus terminology! It will be my life's work. I immediately get started on a mental list: *Peter, Prick, Rod, Demon Stick, Dong, Manhood, Boner, Tool, Schlong, Old Betrayer*—

"Would you fancy a swim?" Noland says, vaporizing my data. But a swim is a sportingly grand idea. The reformed me (struggling to climb back on the wagon) knows I *must* stop dicking around, spit spot. I've got to get out of this penis palace before I do something rash. The sea ought to be safer than a cavern teeming with one-eyed snakes.

"Aye," I say.

I take deep breaths, reminding myself of all the unsexy things that my shrink said lay in wait for me if I don't change my sexy ways: *Loneliness. Alienation from society. Bad credit forever* (though I'm still puzzling over its connection to sex). *Deviance is a symptom of self-hatred,* he'd once said ominously. Why, then, does the deviance factor make the consequences seem so sexy? So *outré?* Why do I so love this feeling of hating myself?

We walk down to the water's edge. I'm not wearing a bathing suit but my underwear and bra could pass as one. Though it's dark, I duck behind a palm tree. Unbuttoning my shirt and my fly in front

---

)

I don't know about you, but my favorite time to appear publicly in a bathing suit is on a moonless night on a secluded beach on a remote island. I didn't always feel like that…say, forty years ago…but now my cellulite is more like celluheavy, and the last Fonda workout I did was with Henry not Jane.

◆

—Phyllis W. Zeno,
"Everybody Out
of the Pool!"

of a man is just too suggestive. For the first time ever I'm not trying to whip myself into any more of a lather than I am in already.

The sea is warm and calm, the glowing clouds of plankton creating a magical soup. I wade in hesitantly, shy. Shylike. Noland grins at me from just beyond, bobbing on the surf. A fetching merman.

"Look at this," says Noland.

He shows me something he'd learned on a trip to West Africa, how to play a water drum. He splashes a Congolese rhumba while I attempt water ballet. We discuss scholarly topics, such as the mating dances of the Trobriand Islanders. After a while, we stop talking and listen to the surf's rise and fall. Inhale, exhale. Diastole, systole. I look down at myself. I am shimmering like a tiny city, glowing with the self-generated light of millions of creatures. I look over at Noland and he's glowing, too, and suddenly I'm aware that his sparkles and mine seem to be calling out to each other, our own little emissaries, our very polite diplomats. *Hello! I see you!* they say. *I see you too!* then bowing to each other, *Thank you* (bow). *No, please, thank you!* For a long time, Noland and I just float, side by side, as tiny alliances are formed between us.

Then Noland mentions he is leaving. He's taking the late boat out of Phranang in a few hours, back to Krabi to catch an all-night bus to Singapore.

Dang.

"I was wondering," he says, "if you'd fancy coming along?"

On rare, perfect days I move through space as if propelled by a benevolent force. No matter where I turn, it is all is so crushingly gorgeous, and my one true purpose is to dip into each shiny poppy bowl and suck nectar like a butterfly, see myself reflected in everything with wide-eyed familiarity. This, according to Shrink #7, is evidence of a narcissistic disorder run so amok, it has its own House of Mirrors. *I am not a narcissist!* I cried, as he nodded and scribbled into his notebook. *What would you say, then, is influencing your behavior?* #7 queried. I thought for a moment. *I'm blinded by science,* I said. He gave me that inscrutable shrink look. I wanted him to understand. *Can't you see?* I said. *I'm caught in a convergence of love and molecules! All that is good inside me is inspired to divide and multiply, a bazillion cells of beneficence splitting off into infinity.*

Noland and I sit under a palm tree, dripping single-celled organisms, while I debate whether or not to abandon the enchanted inlet of Phranang, which I haven't even seen by the light of day. I remind myself that the tsunami wave of lust roaring from the horizons of my veins is not a psychologically sound reason to catch an all-night bus to Singapore with a man I'd just met in a penis cave. I counter that it has to do with *expanding the perfection of the experience,* increasing its chances of staying fixed in my memory without some bum luck busting in and taking over. Like being eaten alive by flophouse bedbugs. Or getting the runs. Or running into those three Aussies in Bangkok, whose vacation pastime is to go from village to village, sampling and comparing prostitutes. If I loiter about this penis voodoo cave much longer, I will likely end up as an instrument of the sea goddess, my sole purpose being to beget more lovers for her enjoyment. Or find myself addicted to the love sparkles in the water, forgetting who I am and where I came from and never, ever be able to leave.

Armed with a dozen rationalizations, I leave at 9 P.M. to catch the all-night bus for Singapore.

I could report how Thais like to watch 2 A.M. machine gun videos on buses that take mountainous turns at 45-degree angles, threatening to pitch themselves into the lush gorges below. I could explain how two people in the back of a bus can share a blanket and feel a sudden chemical reaction take place. I could hypothesize how lust isn't a nasty thing. Or maybe it is. Isn't it about being a pilgrim of the flesh, making devotional offerings to the molecules of another? Molecules that—like those throat singers in Tuva—chant your name and the name of the universe, multitonally, so they sound as one?

It's a scientific theory, anyway, that Noland and I will thoroughly test.

Melinda Misuraca earned an M.F.A. in writing at New College in San Francisco, where she teaches in the graduate writing program. She has completed a collection of short fiction and is at work on a novel.

⋆ ✳ ⋆

Travel Light, Ride Hard

Padded underwear, anyone?

ON MY FIRST TRIP TO CAIRO, I HEADED STRAIGHT FOR the Giza Pyramids with my heart set on a camelback tour. After reading T.E. Lawrence's *Seven Pillars of Wisdom*, I considered myself an expert on all camel-related matters. "Horse better for you, *madame*," the local Bedouins advised flashing golden-toothed smiles. But a horse just did not fit my idea of an exotic desert trek. I had come to the desert and I would ride a camel.

After lengthy negotiations, one of the Bedouins agreed to rent me Habibi, a tall, beautifully adorned male camel (in spite of my insisting pleas for a she-camel—Lawrence would never ride a male, claiming they are stubborn and much more difficult than females). Then, out of a cloud of dust, appeared a skinny dirty little man astride a skinny dirty little horse. "Ali will be your guide," the Bedouin declared, "Ali very good man." My guide's bony face broke into a wide tobacco-stained smile.

I settled as best I could on the large wooden saddle strapped over Habibi's single hump, rearranging the colorful folded blankets used for padding, and careful not to mess up my proud camel's pompoms. As I searched for the non-existent stirrups, Ali encouraged me to ride Bedouin-style, insisting I tuck my right foot under left my left knee (or was it the other way around?) "Lie back," Ali then instructed before clucking his tongue. "What?" I shrieked as Habibi jerked his rear up, nearly catapulting me head first into the sand. Like any self-respecting camel, Habibi had got up by first unfolding his hind legs and then his front legs.

With no harm done, I followed Ali's horse up the first sand dune. "*Ya madame, anti yaani,* you're a natural!" my guide cheered as I cantered smoothly behind him, feeling like a true Bedouin girl, already over-confident. Satisfied, Ali turned around and whipped his horse into a mad gallop he would keep up for much of the ride and that Habibi needed little convincing to imitate.

Until I had mounted Habibi, my riding experience had been limited to about half a dozen horseback rides on beaten trails. I soon discovered that a camel's gallop has nothing to do with a horse's smooth run where you only need to let yourself get carried by the momentum of the horse. I was riding an earthquake! Ali was already too far ahead to hear my desperate cries for help, and Habibi ignored my English, French, and Spanish swears. I remembered Lawrence writing about Bedouin riders who controlled their camel by squeezing its neck between their thighs. With my life depending on my ability to perform fancy Kama Sutra perched atop a twelve-foot-high galloping camel, I searched for other options.

Riding Habibi was like riding an electric bull. Only this wasn't Wild Bill's Rodeo Bar and no one would buy me a beer if I got flung off more than six feet away from my raging mount. Holding on for dear life, I rode around the venerable pyramids with my left hand on the saddle, my right arm stretched up above my head and my shoulders thrown back. With my goofy Gilligan hat and khaki pants, this did not go without entertaining every other rider I met. "Hey! You cowgirl!" one guide shouted through his chuckles, as I raced by him halfway off my saddle, my right arm still up.

Two hours of this led me to a very important conclusion: Thongs are not suitable camel riding apparel. With only thin quick-dry pants between my bare bum and the rough saddle of a galloping camel, I was left looking as if I had slid across a hundred yards of carpet on my bare behind.

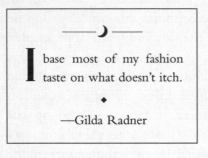

I base most of my fashion taste on what doesn't itch.

♦

—Gilda Radner

In fact, the bruise was so bad that a week later it still had not healed and was threatening to fester. A (sorry) disciple of the "travel light" philosophy, I only carried thongs on my trips. Wearing those would never allow my seeping bruise to heal or even form a scab. I needed full-back cotton underwear.

I ended up shopping for panties in the small Egyptian town of Marsa Matruh. On the main commercial street I first asked a saleswoman where I could find ladies' underwear. It soon became clear that sign language would require me to engage in pantomime unacceptable by any culture's standards. I pulled my travel diary out of my pack and drew a pair of panties for the woman. She smiled knowingly, and wrote down under the picture what I believed was the name of the store where they were sold. She told me to walk up three blocks and to look for a woman in a headscarf.

I walked up three blocks and asked one shopkeeper after another about the underwear store, showing them the lady's inscription in my diary, modestly hiding the panties' picture with my thumb. They all shook their head with a mischievous smile, invariably directing me farther down the road. The last shopkeeper who got to peek at my diary smiled broadly and, with a wink, pinched his hips with his forefingers, mimicking sexy panties. "Yes?" he purred. All color drained from my face as I realized that what that woman had written down in my diary was not the name of the store, but the Arabic word for panties! The shopkeeper signaled for me to follow him and led me to the infamous ladies' underwear store run by an old white-robed man (who also sold ladies' headscarves, hence my confusion).

The old man presented me with a selection of oversized granny undies that seemed to date back to the Second World War. Wearing those, the only male I could ever hope to catch would be of the four-legged kind at best, as I suspect even Habibi would refuse to give me a second look. I settled for two pairs of electric pink and yellow parachutes that set me back a grand total of seventy-five cents. Not a bad investment considering I can wear them again during the last trimester of my first pregnancy.

A week later I was back to wearing thongs. But I never rode a camel again.

Christine Michaud-Martinez has lived, worked, and traveled extensively throughout the Middle East. Her stories have appeared in Sand in My Bra, Whose Panties Are These?, BootsnAll.com, Worldhum.com, *and* Vagabonding.net. *Recently wed to her beloved Cuban amore, she divides her time between Havana and Montreal.*

MICHELLE M. LOTT

* * *

Size Does Matter

But can he get it up and down
without all of us screaming?

I FULLY INTENDED TO GET DOWN TO THE WEIGHT I PUT
on my original driver's license application—someday.

As I recall, I spotted myself five pounds at the time.

Back then, I didn't really think of it as lying per se. To me,
it was more like setting a goal. But, as I splatted out in a vinyl
airport lounge seat, I realized I had yet to reach it. In fact,
judging by the snugness of my waistband, I had probably
raised the bar a little over the years. But I had it covered.
Thanks to my big, beige, but not-too-bulky sweater bal-
looning around me, everything from my neck to just above
my knees was concealed in my own personal khaki cocoon.
With my bulges hidden and overall shape obscured, I looked
like a giant Weeble—a Weeble who clearly favored neutrals.
But no one could see my overgrown parts wobble.

Feeling securely camouflaged, I decided to tackle my ex-
cess tonnage another day, and deal with a bigger problem:
surviving my connecting flight.

Now, I am not really afraid of flying in a plane—it's the

crashing part I'm not so thrilled about. I know it's a fairly pedestrian affair for most people, but the act of defying gravity is not a casual thing for me. Still, experts insist that flying is safer than driving in a car. Which is a small comfort given that I live in Houston, where driving is the city's most popular contact sport.

In my limited flying experience, I have gone through the grab-your-drink, hold-on-tight, and pick-a-religion-any-religion sort of turbulence that simultaneously tests your cardiac, digestive, and bladder functions. I have also been stuck on the ground in a plane for upwards of two hours in the Texas summer heat, because—it was announced after the first hour or so—they were having trouble getting the door closed. I am not kidding. I consider it a badge of honor that I stayed on that plane. But it was big and full of people, and I still believe there's safety in numbers.

Which is why I do feel pretty safe flying, actually. As long as I'm on a huge, hulking monster of an airliner, I tend to have lots of company. You see, I figure the Big Guy upstairs can aim his magnifying glass at cars and pick them off like ants with nary a second thought. But with airplanes, he's got to think long and hard before he decides to let a whole load of passengers go down.

Of course, this theory goes out the window once you get on a little plane. Logically, if you look at them, you would think size alone would give them a great advantage over large jets. After all, they are smaller and lighter, and you would think it would be a whole lot easier to keep them up there. You would think that, but you would be wrong.

Just watch the news, and you will quickly recognize that little planes are the mobile homes of the aviation world. The Big Guy seems to enjoy watching them get tossed and thrown around like ice in a blender. Which is why people refer to them euphemistically as puddle jumpers, worm burners—or connecting flights. It just sounds better than crapshoot commuters.

When I made my reservation, I thoroughly questioned the ticket agent as to the nature of the aircraft involved. I wanted assurance that the plane was of substantial size and construction. That it did not come out of a box. That duct tape and paper were not part of its structural integrity. That it could not in any way be described as "cute" or "little" or "tiny," as in "Awwww, what a shame that cute little tiny plane got smashed into such cute little tiny pieces." That it was a plane that he, himself, would actually feel quite comfortable flying on—along with all that he valued in this life: his dog, his big screen TV, and, perhaps, assorted loved ones.

The agent convinced me that yes, he would indeed board the same aircraft I would be flying on without hesitation—due to its significant strength, remarkable reliability, and, of course, its fairly elephantine proportions.

The prop plane I got on reminded me, once again, that men are prone to bouts of uncommon generosity when it comes to the comparative dimensions of certain things. Because my plane was, well, uh, much smaller than I expected. Frankly, it looked like a slightly more aerodynamic form of a Ford Pinto.

I tried to remain calm. All told, there were maybe four or five passengers, plus a flight attendant. We could have easily fit in a rental car and completely forgotten about this coffin with wings.

To rid my brain of thoughts of imminent peril and pain, I settled into the comfort of my baggy sweater and concentrated on a lighter subject: my plan for a less expansive version of myself—assuming I made it back home. I imagined the salads I would eat. The desserts I would politely turn down. I saw myself sweating off the parasites that had attached themselves to my body: *Abdominis poochis*, *Hippus hippopotami*, and *Arsus huges*.

The flight attendant interrupted my visions of the newer, thinner, non-parasitized me with a jolting request. Before we could take off, it seemed someone had to volunteer to move to a different seat to balance out the weight of the plane.

This is absolutely true.

Well, I panicked like Jenny Craig caught sneaking into a Krispy Kreme shop.

Were we all going to die because I still had five—O.K., ten—pounds to lose? Was it finally catching up to me after all these years?

Everyone else seemed stunned, too. It's not every day that attention is so pointedly and publicly directed at your body mass—collective though it may be. Perhaps we were all thinking the same thing: maybe Twinkies really can kill you. Maybe that brownie binge was going to do us in. Maybe we all had to answer to our maker for every extra slice of pizza.

Finally, some brave soul got up and moved. I didn't have the nerve to turn around to look to see who it was. I was too ashamed of myself. And my girth.

The flight attendant seemed satisfied that we were ready to go.

I held my breath all the way to my destination.

For what it's worth, during the beverage service, I requested water. And I did not eat the cookie that came with it.

But, I did do a lot of thinking on that flight. I decided it was time to make peace with the fifteen pounds I had put on. Life is just not worth living without a certain amount of cheese and chocolate to get you through.

We landed safely back on earth, and I had survived my

little trip on Just Lucky I Guess Airways. And that was cause enough to eat my cookie in celebration. From then on, I vowed it would be jumbo jets or nothing. Because when it comes to planes—along with certain other things—bigger is definitely better.

Michelle Lott lives in Houston, Texas with three cats and a dog. A veterinarian by trade, she turned to writing when her pets grew tired of listening to her stories. Her love of cheese and chocolate remains boundless, and she refuses to seek help for it.

*

Not long after having major back surgery, I decided to travel. I flew to Palm Springs in first class, the extra room being just what I needed. A few days later, my onward flight to Las Vegas in a smaller plane had no first class, so I had to fly economy on what promised to be a full flight. We were originally scheduled to depart at 4:25 P.M., but a series of automated phone alerts told me the flight would be delayed until 5:40, then 6:30, and finally 7:15. By sheer happenstance, I checked the flight status online at 5:30, only to learn that the flight had been changed *back* to 6:45. I raced through commute traffic to the airport to find the terminal empty. Where was everyone?

I made it to the gate just in time to board, but I was the only one in the boarding area, for a flight I knew was nearly booked because of the seat choices available at the time I booked my ticket. The gate agent informed the crew that the passengers were ready to load—all one of them. When I looked questioningly at her, she said that due to the delay half the booked passengers had been bused to Ontario Airport for a direct flight, and the other half had rented cars and driven. The impatience of these people allowed me to have a once-in-a-lifetime experience—I had the whole plane to myself! All those automated phone calls and the mad dash to the airport had rewarded little old me with a private jet and my very own personal stewardess.

—Susan Brady, "Celebrity for a Flight"

* * *

Heave-Ho

It's up the mountain with Chuck we go.

FOR WEEKS IN FRANCE, I FELT LIKE THE CARTOON RABBIT in the Trix commercials who almost gets the cereal before it's snatched away. "Silly American, France is for sophisticated people!" I imagined being scolded in that sing-song voice each time I mangled a simple French word, wore the wrong outfit to a restaurant, or did the cheek-kiss thing only twice instead of four times.

But here at the finish line for a Tour de France stage in the Pyrenees mountains, surrounded by bicycles and booze, I was as close to being in my element as I'd ever been in France. Sitting with my bike on a grassy hill in front of the giant TV broadcasting the race, plastic cup of wine in one hand, cheese in the other, it was easier to pretend that I blended in with the Europeans around me.

When American Lance Armstrong crossed the finish line first, taking possession of the prestigious yellow jersey from French cyclist Francois Simon, my boyfriend and I cheered politely, but not too loudly, with the rest of the crowd.

However, the American college boys in front of us, wearing matching blue U.S. Postal cycling caps and baggy khaki shorts, let loose. One shook a bottle of champagne, and after a brief struggle, popped the cork, spraying his friends and some of the nearby crowd.

"Whoo-hooooo!" he yelled as he doused his buddy. "Take THAT, ya Frenchies!"

Not to be outdone, the other guy pumped his fist in the air. "Yeah!" he shouted. "*Yeah!*"

A few people nearby looked at the boys and sighed. "*Americans,*" they seemed to say wearily, before ignoring them. Rolling my eyes, I sighed too, hoping that my American accent had gone unnoticed.

"Tourists," I said under my breath like an insult. For once, I wasn't the one committing a *faux pas*. I looked at Bob and smiled.

"What?"

"They should know better," I said smugly as we started riding down the mountain. But my self-satisfaction soon faded as the altitude, sun, and alcohol took their toll. I was dehydrated, and was quickly developing a headache. Exhaust fumes from the hundreds of vehicles stuck in a traffic jam on the mountain road saturated the air, and my little headache sprouted like a pop-up sponge.

When we got to the town of Arreau, just before we were to ride over another mountain pass, I realized I couldn't go any farther. I collapsed on a bench in a quiet square near the center of town while Bob went to find aspirin. He returned with a round white pill nearly the size of my fist and a glass of water.

"Were you at the pharmacy or the veterinarian's?" I asked.

"It's like Alka-Seltzer," Bob explained as we watched the pill dissolve into a mass of fizzy bubbles in the glass.

It can't be that bad, I thought as I gulped down the mixture. By the time Bob returned the glass to the pharmacist and came back, I was feeling better and willing to try riding again. Bob, however, had other plans.

"We're going to hitchhike," he announced.

Great. I've never liked hitchhiking because of the rejection. Plus, there's the pressure to perform. When accepting a ride from a stranger, I've always felt like I've entered into an unwritten pact: it's the driver's job to provide the transportation, and it's my duty to provide polite but engaging conversation, leaving the kindly stranger with a good story to tell friends back home.

"I can make it over the pass. Let's just ride," I pleaded.

Bob shook his head. "You'll never make it." I knew he was right.

A steady stream of traffic was headed over the pass to the next day's race course. I smiled and tried not to look sick as I held out my thumb. Elderly couples driving big RVs eyed us suspiciously and sped past or avoided eye contact all together. Younger couples in European two-seaters drove by and shrugged "sorry" at us. This wasn't working.

It shouldn't be this difficult for a Lycra-wearing blonde to get a ride, I thought. I glanced at Bob. He hadn't shaved in a couple days and he looked like the hippies we saw in the grocery store stealing dog food by stuffing the bags down their oversized pants. We were not conveying the wholesome image I wanted to project.

"Here, stand back a bit," I told Bob as I smiled at the next car. The driver slowed and pulled over.

We introduced ourselves. The man was Dutch. "We have bikes," I apologized. "But look! They'll easily fit in your trunk!" I knew I was being too cheerful, desperately so, but I couldn't stop speaking in exclamations.

"I know, I know," the man said impatiently. "I saw the bikes—that's why I stopped."

Once we were on our way, I turned on the charm. Holding up my end of the hitchhiking bargain, I asked the man's teenaged son, sitting in the front seat, about school. As the car wound up the twisting mountain road, I tried to make interesting comments about the Tour de France, but I started to get queasy. Horrified, I realized I was getting car sick. I looked over at Bob for help with the conversation, but he was staring out the window at the mountains.

I leaned forward, pretending to sit closer up front so I could have a more intimate conversation with the driver, but I really just wanted to concentrate on a steady spot on the horizon. When we went around another sharp corner, I realized if I did get sick, I'd barf into the front seat directly between the man and his son. I might as well rob them and slash their tires while I was at it, and then I could officially become the worst hitchhiker ever. My stomach rolled.

"I don't feel very well," I whispered to Bob.

We'd been traveling together long enough for Bob to know exactly what that meant. In one smooth motion, he emptied his small backpack and handed it to me for use as a vomit receptacle. Not wanting to throw up in the backpack, I put my hand up to my mouth, hoping that I'd discreetly spit up whatever was in my stomach and catch it in my cupped palm. My stomach convulsed. When I started to throw up, Bob calmly reached across me to open the car door. I stuck my head out of the moving vehicle and barfed on the road as the driver slowed to a stop. A line of cars were stuck behind us on the narrow road, unable to navigate around my head sticking out of the open door.

With nothing left in my stomach, I started heaving. I was not holding up my end of the hitchhiking bargain. Awful retching noises emerged from deep in my gut, and there was apparently no end to them. The cars behind us started to get impatient. Someone honked. No, this wasn't charming at all. *There's nothing left!* I told my stomach in desperation. *Stop it. Just stop it!*

I started to think about how I had probably ruined this man's belief in being kind to hitchhikers—he might never pick up another hitchhiker again. I felt so bad about this, the retching actually intensified. Now, several cars were honking. European girls probably never took this long to throw up. I didn't want to be just another American behaving badly abroad, but I was.

When it was over, I took a deep breath, pulled my head back in the car, and closed the door. The driver looked at me in the rearview mirror, eyebrows raised. "I'm done," I announced.

"And now that you got it out, you feel better?" the man asked. His son looked at me, alarmed.

"Oh, yes!" I said cheerfully, falling back into my happy hitchhiker persona. "Much better!"

The man hadn't asked, but I felt I had to tell him anyway. "I didn't get any in the car, you know."

He didn't seem to be worried about it. He shrugged a little, as if to say either way was fine with him. "That is quite something!" he told me. "Now you can say you spit up on the famous Col d'Aspen, the route of the Tour de France!"

Be cool, be cool, I thought. "Yes," I agreed. "That is quite something. So what's the weather like in the Netherlands in the fall?" We started chatting about rain.

The man dropped us off at the town where we were staying. I made it out of the car and over to the side of the road by the campground, barely waiting for him to drive away before I started hurling again. As I leaned on the guardrail, I was vaguely aware of a nearby couple who were eating dinner in front of their camper. Bob struck up a conversation with them, and between spasms of barfing, I was dismayed to overhear their nationalities. For the second time in one day, I was throwing up in front of more nice Dutch people. I started making the horrible retching noises as the couple continued eating. To distract them, Bob turned the conversation to the politics of the Tour de France.

I was grateful that Bob had taken over the entertaining duties and was doing his best to charm his new-found friends. It was a little odd, though, how no one seemed to mind that I was doing so much throwing up. I wondered if it was common for Americans to puke in front of the Dutch. Perhaps this sort of thing, like the college boys earlier, was to be expected and ignored, much in the same way one would ignore a cute, but improperly trained puppy.

Instead of fighting it, I decided to accept the situation. I would just ride out the heaving as gracefully as possible. My mind started to wander. I heaved again, and thought about how my abs were going to be sore the next day—they hadn't gotten a workout like this in ages.

The Dutch couple still seemed oblivious to my awful behavior. God bless the Dutch! And then, like an athlete in her finest moment, I had a flash of clarity where everything faded to the background and I knew what I had to do. I took a deep breath, and the heaving stopped.

I stumbled, exhausted, over to where Bob was still talking with the Dutch couple. They chatted with me about the weather for a few minutes before sending us off with their map and best wishes. I was kidding myself to think that I'd ever fit in here in France—I'd always be just another awkward American. But in the Netherlands, well, perhaps that's where my not-so-graceful attempts at socializing and my tendency towards car sickness might go unnoticed, if today was any indication.

"So, Bob, what do you think about going to Amsterdam?"

Jennifer Colvin has traveled extensively with her husband Bob, who has been faithfully by her side while she's gotten car sick, bus sick, train sick, and gondola sick in a variety of countries. Her stories have been appeared in various print and online publications, including the anthologies Sand in My Bra *and* A Women's Europe. *Between trips, she lives and works in the San Francisco Bay Area.*

JULIA WEILER

* ✱ *

R-Rated Rescue

Wonder Woman puts the "ass"
back in assistance.

I AM A VETERINARY TECHNICIAN AND INCURABLE
bleeding-heart, so travel presents me with a unique problem.
Even while on the road, I am unable to let go of my inex-
orable desire to heal every broken, sick, needy, or otherwise
pathetic creature that has the good fortune to cross my path.
If the animal happens to be feline, my desire to aid the distressed creature is especially relentless. I keep a veterinary first
aid kit in my backpack for this reason and will do almost anything to help a cat, sometimes even to the point of faux pas.

During several glorious weeks on a small island in the
gulf of Thailand, I set out for a day hike with my husband
and a few friends. We had barely covered any ground when
we came across a most upsetting sight. On the steps of a
beachside café in the baking sun, a small black cat lay
parched in the heat. She was sick, injured, and dying alone.
Tiny armies of biting ants rifled through her fur and crept
into her ears and nostrils. Her obvious pre-mortem suffering
tore at my soul.

"Not much you can do for that one," someone in the group offered, eager to end the interruption. That might be true, I thought, but I needed to at least try, and if nothing else I could offer her a more peaceful passing. I scooped up the limp, little cat and wrapping her in a sarong headed home. Back at my rustic bungalow, just feet from the water's edge, I sat on the veranda and assessed my patient's condition. With my trusty vet-bag at my side and a reluctant husband as assistant I began my work.

A few hours later the "project cat," as my travel mates had labeled her, was alert and could even hold her head up. Although she still had a fight ahead of her, life seemed to be back on her side. Knowing that she would be a long-term patient I set up a blanket for her inside the bungalow. This activity and its consequence did not, to say the least, please my husband. Although he had shown honorable patience in my undertaking, he drew the line at sharing our sleeping quarters with a sick, flea-ridden cat that couldn't control her bladder.

Despite an impassioned though squeaky protest, I lost the ensuing battle and pouted my way outside to see what accommodations I could provide on the veranda. The area was enclosed by a railing except for a small opening at the top of the stairs. My concern was protecting the little cat from any nocturnal intruders, namely the beach dogs who had probably caused her current predicament. Determined to prevent any canine invasions, I built a barricade of rattan chairs to block the entrance until morning. Confident in my modifications, I moved my patient outside and tucked her snugly into bed.

After double-checking the perimeter for safety, I ducked back inside the bungalow to bed down for the night. Hot and tired from the day, I stripped down to my birthday suit and sought refuge in the comforts of my mosquito net–draped bed. As I crawled under the covers next to my husband, we giggled over the day's adventure and the good fortunes of "project cat." Amends made, I drifted off to sleep as sounds of the ocean waves soothed my subconscious. All was calm, yet somewhere in the dark distance the faint sound of barking dogs whispered an ominous premonition.

Early the next morning, not long after sunrise, I awoke to streams of glorious sunshine cascading through my windows. As I drew in the sweet splendors of waking up in paradise, I was jolted suddenly from my tropical bliss. I remembered my patient on the veranda as a cold, sickening sensation of something about to go wrong chilled me. It was then that I heard it, the loud crash of my barricade coming down followed by the deafening roar of angry dogs.

I bolted up in bed throwing covers haphazardly to the side. I leapt from the sheets and in the process, became entangled in the mosquito netting. As I struggled to get free I glanced at my husband in hope of assistance, but still fast asleep, he remained ignorant of the disaster in progress. After several agonizing and unassisted seconds, I was free and on my feet. I sprinted towards the door and, in my haste, was as unaware of my disposition as my husband seemed to be of the ruckus on the veranda.

I raced outside and stopped only to grab a rattan chair, which I waved menacingly above my head like a fierce tribal warrior. There must have been at least five dogs on the veranda, all of which were drooling and intent on having cat for breakfast. Teeth bared and growling, the mangy beasts threatened violence. I could see the little cat frozen in the corner, her eyes the size of saucers. She seemed to utter a silent prayer as she quickly counted the number of lives she had left. The dogs edged closer. I jumped protectively in front of the little cat just in the nick of time.

The frothy-mouthed mongrels had us surrounded on three sides, but in my mother bear's fury, the pack was no match for me. "BAAAD DOGS," I screamed while I swung the chair and fended them off like a crazed lion tamer. "Wax on, Wax off," my inner-karate-kid hollered as I spun and high-kicked the air. Whizzing and turning, my hair flying wildly, I held the dogs off one after another until at last, whimpering in defeat, they were gone. Euphoric, I felt like a super hero. I was Wonder Woman…Super Girl…The Feline Avenger…I was…CLICK CLICK…teehee…Errr…what was that???

My reverie was quickly disrupted by a growing cacophony of strange yet familiar sounds. CLICK…CLICK… WHZZZ…teehee. My adrenaline began to recede and a weird sinking feeling steadily took its place as a cool morning breeze registered on a patch of flesh not normally exposed to weather. I realized then that in my race to the rescue, I had neglected to put on any clothes. I was bare-ass naked. CLICK…WHZZ…tee heehee.

I reluctantly turned towards the noise. To my horror, there just fourteen feet in front of me in the small lagoon beyond my veranda, a large group of giggling Japanese tourists stood ankle-deep in the water. They were armed with every type of camera or video recording device imaginable; all of which were pointing right at me. Disrupted from their tidal pool explorations by my burlesque spectacle, they had captured the entire show on film. Still snapping away, they apparently expected an encore.

CLICK…WHZZZ…teehee.

I picked up the cat and showed the poor bedridden feline to my audience as if this would explain my ridiculous behavior. "See, I saved this dear, little kitten from those killer dogs. I'm not nuts...it was an EMERGENCY." My attempt at communication only fueled their now explosive laughter. CLICK...CLICK...teehee. Chagrined, desperate, and painfully aware of my nudity, I did next what any good, feline-rescuing, exhibitionist, kung fu fighting, super hero would do...a modest curtsy followed by an immediate exit.

As I backed into the bungalow, gingerly holding the cat as a makeshift modesty shield, I turned to notice my husband standing at the window. "Can you believe that just happened?" I asked him incredulously.

"What I can't believe is that you ran out there naked," he replied casually. As I was about to react to his maddening remark, I noticed that he was munching a handful of honey-roasted peanuts as though he'd been watching a movie. "Chomp...chomp...crunch...I mean, DIDN'T YOU SEE ALL THOSE PEOPLE?" he added, "They were taking pictures you know." I shot him my best Persist-And-You-Shall-Die look as I prepared a bed for the cat indoors.

Over time my patient enjoyed a full recovery, and a few days before we left the island, a German woman who owned a shop there sweetly offered to adopt the little cat. Giving her up was difficult, but I knew she would have a happy, canine-free environment in which she could safely explore the remainder of her nine lives. I gratefully accepted the offer and on our last day tearfully handed her over. As we said our final goodbyes, the shop owner requested that I pose with my former patient for a snapshot memento. I happily agreed and proudly held the little cat in my arms, but as I smiled for the camera, I felt for just a brief moment, overdressed for the occasion. CLICK...teehee.

Julia Weiler has done everything from schlepping gourmet coffee to working in the veterinary field, but these days you will find her behind a camera, trying her hand at documentary filmmaking. When not filming, editing, or researching, she enjoys scuba diving, kayaking, surfing, hiking, gardening, and any excuse to travel.

ANN LOMBARDI

* * *

Mein Gott, I've Fried His Underpants

Living a dream in Switzerland, mostly.

AFTER THREE MONTHS OF BLITZ BACKPACKING ALL over Europe, I couldn't wait to reach Switzerland, the perfect refuge for my travel-weary bones. My return flight home from Zurich was three weeks away, and visions of tranquil pastures, alpine lakes, and creamy chocolates danced in my head. How could I pass up the alluring *"Ferien Auf Dem Bauernhof"* (Farm Vacation) program touted in the tourist office brochures? I was sure it would be a cross-cultural eye-opener for this city slicker, housework-challenged American. So, I plopped down a finder's fee, scooped up the address of my host farm family, and hopped a train to the country for my long-awaited taste of rural life.

Rolf and Ruth Sprunger welcomed me into their 400-year-old farmhouse, nestled high in the hills of Basel-land. The tiny village was a good hour's walk, through vast forests and fields, from the town of Liestal. And the old farm? It was the place of my dreams: a contented menagerie of dairy cows with huge hand-painted bells, horses, pigs, hens, goats, and a half dozen assorted dogs and cats. I delighted in the bountiful cherry and apple trees, organic veggie gardens, and the best homemade hazelnut carrot cake this side of the Atlantic.

The dark, worn wooden floors with secrets of centuries creaked musically throughout the house. A heavenly aroma of freshly baked wholegrain bread floated room-to-room from the wood-burning kitchen oven. I was in my element, and honestly didn't miss any of my usual creature comforts, like central heating or upstairs toilets. For those brisk autumn nights, I already had mastered the art of starting the fire in my very own bedroom furnace and warming up the nifty mini-pillows filled with cherry pits, which kept my feet toasty under the fluffy goose down quilt. I was intrigued. Such an uncomplicated, peaceful existence! This truly was life the way it was meant to be, I thought, as I drifted off to sleep.

I have to admit, though, there was one habit of the meticulous Swiss I found impossible to understand. For some odd reason, the Sprunger family had an obsession with ironing anything made of cloth, including every imaginable item of clothing worn by their army of children...fourteen of the rascals, to be exact. Who ever heard of pressing denim work coveralls, or heaven help us, bed linens!? Now this was really going overboard with the Martha Stewart thing. Naturally one of my daily chores was to tackle those mammoth piles of ironing, a job I truly dreaded. To my credit, however, I never once complained, reminding myself that hard work builds character.

One afternoon on a particularly gorgeous autumn day, I plotted to finish my ironing duties in record time. No numb hands and fingers for me today! Nor was I about to stay cooped up indoors with such beautiful weather beckoning me out to nature. Halfway through my ironing at the bottom of one pile, I spotted three pairs of the fanciest men's underpants I had ever laid eyes on. They were those skimpy, low-cut European ones made of nylon net, the kind no red-blooded American male I know would ever be caught dead wearing. I immediately guessed the fancy briefs had been inside that festively wrapped birthday package a giggling Frau Sprunger had presented her hubby just a few days before. Of course I realized instinctively these underpants were not to be ironed. Carefully folding all three pairs in the precise Swiss manner I had been taught (in thirds, with the fronts facing up), I carefully laid them aside on the ironing board while I continued to plug away.

Seconds later the family Saint Bernard bolted in out of nowhere, scaring the bejeevers out of me. I froze, too stunned to react to the mushroom cloud of foul-smelling smoke growing bigger by the minute. *Mein Gott*, I had knocked over the scalding iron! It had hit the prized skivvies dead center. My first impulse was to run. Regaining my composure, I managed to unplug the hissing iron, grab a kitchen spatula, and frantically scrape the iron's underside. My efforts were in vain. A sticky glob of melted, charred nylon was plastered all over the bottom. And worse, the underpants were ruined, hopelessly welded together at what used to be the crotches. I decided then and there not to say a word to the Sprungers; that is, not until I had bought both a new iron and underwear. Thankfully, the next day Lady Luck took pity on me, and amazingly enough, I found the perfect replacements. Somehow I just never got around to fessing up to Herr and Frau Sprunger. Why spoil a relaxing vacation?

My memorable farm stint came to a close all too soon. The last day of my stay, I received a surprise farewell present from Mr. and Mrs. Sprunger. It was a lovely Swiss travel scrapbook with a handwritten note inscribed "To our favorite American visitor." Touched by their thoughtfulness, I peeked inside the album. My jaw dropped. On the very first page were a sketched smiley-faced iron...and a neatly glued chunk of Herr Sprunger's fried underpants.

Ann Lombardi is a twenty-two-year veteran travel consultant and former E.S.L. teacher with a knack for misadventure. Ann's zest for travel has lured her to Europe, South and Central America, Asia, and the Caribbean. Among her fondest exploits are crashing on a runaway Lapp reindeer sled, being trapped in a phone booth during an alpine blizzard, finishing dead last in the Berlin Marathon, bailing out of a glider plane near Bern, hitching a ride on an Amish horse and buggy, touring Moscow with a black marketer, and getting tear-gassed in curlers outside a Seoul hair salon. She hangs her backpack in Atlanta, Georgia, and you can find out more about her at TheTripChicks.com.

* ✳ *

Killing Me Softly
with Your Stare

Do I know you?

On a lop-sided ramshackle bus
We ride from day to day
We bounce and we bump
As we rattle along, we rattle along our way…

I JUST COULDN'T GET RID OF THIS TUNE. IT KEPT
playing over and over in my head. I had clambered into this
rickety bus to see the magnificent Mysore Palace and the
famous gold throne. A five-hour journey from Bangalore, in
South India, would take me to the smaller town of Mysore.

I knew there was something wrong. It was not just the
slippery-looking, skinny guy who had donned a dazzling red
polyester shirt and tight "Levy" jeans (yes, this was the label).
True, he was gaping at me and I was uncomfortable with his
unwanted attention. But, there was something else that was
amiss and I could not place my finger on it.

I shrugged off my feeling of unease and settled into a
window seat. I plugged in my Walkman, partly to drown the

silly ditty still resounding in my head, and decided to make the best of it. My cold stares kept the "polyester" man away from the middle row where I had seated myself.

I soon knew what was wrong, or at least I thought I did. As a luxury air-conditioned coach overtook us on the dusty road, belching smoke as it shot past us, I knew I had made a big mistake. This bus, in which I was seated, was not for tourists. It was a regular state transport bus, which plied at frequent intervals between Bangalore and Mysore and ferried locals.

Anyway, even if I was not on the luxury coach we were definitely moving towards Mysore. Having recently shifted to Bangalore, this was my first trip in South India and I was looking forward to a glimpse of the royal splendor. For now, the only splendor on display were the colorful dresses worn by the schoolgirls. However, the dazzling red polyester shirt was an aberration.

There were more than a handful of schoolgirls on this bus. As schoolgirls anywhere in the world are prone to, they were all giggling happily and sharing secrets. All of them wore bright blue long skirts and colorful blouses. These blouses either sported bright floral patterns or were in shades of bright green, pink, yellow, purple, and orange.

The only other woman traveler on this bus, slightly plump and perhaps in her early thirties, sported a green-and-orange sari—the traditional wrap-around garment worn by women in India. Beautiful multicolored glass bangles jangled pleasantly on her wrists, and she wore some delicate white flowers around her hair-bun.

I looked quite drab in comparison. All I had on was gray cotton trousers and an equally drab gray t-shirt. But my digital wristwatch that sported a bright yellow plastic strap helped me from fading into the background altogether. It was also my lucky charm.

This wristwatch was a gift from a fellow traveler. We had braved a blizzard in the Himalayan region and made it safely to base camp. The watch was now worn out and battered; still I never traveled without it.

People watching is fun and it helped me to kill time. Suddenly the ditty that was still playing in my head died down. My brain was alert, my body tensed. I had just spotted the sign: Welcome to the Bandipur Forest Region.

I normally would have craned my neck to spot the *chital* (spotted deer) that frolicked close to the road. But the hair on the nape of my neck was now standing up. I could feel the goosebumps on my skin. Bandipur wasn't just a paradise for wildlife enthusiasts. It was Veerappan land.

Veerappan was wanted in the southern states of India for killing more than one hundred people, including senior police and forest officials. Anyone who tried to come in the way of his flourishing business of smuggling sandalwood or poaching elephants was dealt with mercilessly. He had even abducted and killed a former minister and also kidnapped a famous movie star from his farmhouse on the outskirts of this forest region, only to release him later (the saying goes that the release was made only against a hefty ransom). The Bandipur forest region abounded in sandalwood trees and still teemed with herds of elephants. It was Veerappan's favorite haunt.

I had seen his photographs in the local newspapers so many times I could recognize that handlebar mustache anywhere. He was very proud of his moustache and tended to it carefully. Newspapers reported that he waxed and groomed it almost daily. To him, it was a sign of his manliness. This together with his piercing black eyes made for a very fierce portrait. He lorded over this region. I was mad. Mad not to have checked out the route to Mysore. I had never even dreamed that this bus would take me through this dangerous area.

As an accountant, I have always been partial to statistics. I remembered Veerappan's details vividly; it was almost like I was reading aloud from a newspaper. Ivory smuggled worth U.S. $2.6 million, sandalwood carted off around 10,000 tons worth a whopping U.S. $22 million. The price on Veerappan's head, a cool U.S. $1 million plus!

I looked around the bus. The "polyester" man had stopped whistling and combing his mop of well-oiled hair. The farmers, who had sprawled comfortably on the seats and were scattered here and there, were no longer speaking across to each other in their local Kannada dialect. The two schoolgirls seated just ahead of me were peering outside the window wide-eyed.

It was unbelievable. I never could have imagined that this noisy bunch of fellow travelers could ever keep quiet, except perhaps when in deep slumber. Now, if even one of the delicate white flowers, which my fellow woman traveler adorned, had fallen off, we would have all heard it—loud and clear. It was eerie. Now I knew the meaning of pin-drop silence.

Our bus screeched to a sudden halt. The driver shot out some sharp commands. I did not understand a word of what he was saying. People were filing out quietly. I had to follow suit. All I knew was that it wasn't a case of a measly tire puncture or engine failure. It was something much, much worse. The queasy feeling in the pit of my stomach told me so. I wish I knew what it was. Well, actually I had no wish to know what had happened.

For once, I dreamed of being in my cubicle, hunched over the laptop. Bored to death but safe and sound. But there I was, standing with others on the forest ground. If someone invented a pill to quash the travel bug, I knew I would be the first to queue up to be a human guinea pig.

A forest official began to scrutinize each and every face very closely. When it was my turn, the guy yelled at me, in Kannada, I presume. He tried again, in another language— perhaps it was Tamil. Several languages, all unknown to me, are widely spoken in South India. This official then just threw up his hands in a helpless gesture.

It was the "polyester" man who explained to me in a smattering of English that Veerappan had stirred some fresh trouble. Entry farther down in this area was forbidden, our bus would have to turn back to Bangalore.

Clutching my backpack tightly, as if it would bring me some solace, I climbed back into the bus. The "polyester" man did not clamber back, he remained behind to enjoy the fun, I suppose. Or perhaps to act as the interpreter for other poor souls like me. My only connection with the world had slipped away. The chatting began; the farmers were talking loudly, as were the bus driver and ticket collector. One of the schoolgirls began to sob. The sari-clad woman rushed to her aid and hugged her. I wish she had hugged me as well. I felt so alone, so aloof. It was like being stranded in a desert.

But I steeled myself. I wasn't a school kid. I had traveled alone in other regions of India, regions considered inhospitable to a solo woman traveler. Surely I could brave this ride back to Bangalore. I thought of taking a quick nap. But, grabbing some shut-eye was just not possible. I was as wide-eyed and scared shitless as the school kids.

I knew I was shivering, but I tried to pretend that I was tuned in to my Walkman and was swaying to the music.

The bus made a U-turn. We were going back, the way we had come, back to Bangalore. The only hitch—we had forayed deep down into the forest area. It would be at least half an hour before we hit the main road and civilization. Not good, not good at all.

On the way back, the driver stopped, it seemed every few minutes, to pick up passersby, rural folk, who had no idea that they could not venture deeper down the road into the forested area.

Till now the bus had been largely empty. But now it was getting crowded. More and more people got in. People with jute sacks filled with grain, people carrying bundles of sugar cane, stacks of hay or firewood, and even piles of clothes. Perhaps this person with a huge bundle of clothes was a shop owner.

No one sat next to me. Perhaps it was my smelly socks, or the fright that was visible on my face. Or did they just want someone to talk to?

I realized I had been uncivil enough to dump my backpack on the seat next to mine. With a sigh, I moved it beneath the bus seat. Another stop and crowds of people shoved their way in.

And then it happened. Someone dropped himself heavily into the seat next to mine. I turned to look. It was a tall wiry man with a fierce handlebar mustache. I gaped openmouthed. He wore the traditional *dhoti* (white cloth wrapped around his waist), an extremely tattered vest, and a loose overcoat of some kind. There was something hidden beneath his overcoat.

Beads of sweat appeared on my forehead and trickled

down. I began to shudder. My heart was thudding so hard I thought it would jump out. I began to edge towards the window, wishing I could leap out of it. There was no doubt about it. This man was the one and only Veerappan.

What was Veerappan hiding beneath his overcoat? Elementary, my dear Watson, what could it be besides arms and ammunition. Perhaps it was a country-made pistol, a dagger? Or if nothing else, perhaps an extra-sharp sickle?

No, it looked like he was hiding a handmade grenade. Only a grenade would be much smaller. It was a country-made bomb. Yes, that was it, a bomb. What if it suddenly exploded? The heat was unbearable; didn't country made bombs explode in the heat? Both he and I would instantly die. He would not even have to take the pains to kill me.

To make matters worse, another ditty began to resound loudly in my head, only this time, it was my own creation— "Dead as a dodo, dead as a duck, as dead as you on a trundling bus." What an unusual trip. My unique dance moves to begin with and now my own ditty!

The masses of people that had just got in with Veerappan blocked my view of the driver. Was the driver held at gunpoint? Where was the bus going? Once again, a deep hush seemed to descend. The woman traveler heaved herself up, it seemed to be as far away from me as possible, and disappeared ahead in the standing crowd. Others shot sly glances in my direction, or so it seemed. The pounding of my heart could not get any worse. My t-shirt was already soaked in sweat.

I wanted to call my mother. But each time I tried to dive down and pull out my backpack, where my mobile phone lay buried amidst clothes and books, sharp black eyes would follow me.

I didn't want to be abducted; I didn't want to be slashed with a knife, either. I began to believe in karma. I was just destined to die on a trundling bus.

I glanced at my wrist to check the time. Veerappan followed my gaze. Worse still, he continued to stare at my wrist, as the seconds and minutes went by. I was done for, he was going to grab me and slash my wrist. In fact, I had caught him glancing at my wrist even earlier. Perhaps that big ugly bulge was not a country bomb, it was a sharp dagger.

Veerappan suddenly reached into his overcoat. Now I would either be killed or taken hostage. I began to shiver even more violently than ever, my teeth chattered. I could not figure out what would be worse—having my wrists slashed or being his hostage. From Veerappan's perspective, the only apparent city slicker on this bus would command a bigger ransom. So perhaps I would not be killed. The police authorities would not like to send a signal that even visitors, let alone, officials were being kidnapped and killed by Veerappan as they watched helplessly. Surely the state government would succeed in securing my release. Maybe I could escape. Would watching Tarzan help me survive, if ever I did escape? Could I swing on trees? Would I be a national hero, after having escaped Veerappan?

As I was thinking all this and much worse, Veerappan drew out a large crumpled paper packet—the bulge beneath his overcoat had disappeared. He shyly nudged me and offered me roasted peanuts. I didn't know whether to laugh or cry.

And why was he staring at me so hard, each time I had tried to dive for my backpack? During our trip, as he eventually pointed at my wristwatch and grinned a tobacco-stained, toothy smile, I understood. He had not seen anything like it before and he loved my watch.

Perhaps the fast-changing digits fascinated him, or perhaps yellow was his favorite color. When we finally made it back to the bus station at Bangalore, and I was not as dead as a dodo, even though dead tired, I gave him my watch. I wonder whether he still wears it.

Lubna Kably calls herself a wondering wanderer. Her adventures of traveling in India have appeared on www.bootsnall.com. Today she roams freely in the forests of Bandipur and other parts of India, in search of another misadventure. The real Veerappan was killed in a police encounter in 2004, after having evaded arrest for nearly twenty years.

LAURA KLINE

* ✱ *

Bathtub Blues in the Land of the Rising Buns

Were they plumbers or perverts?

MY GOOD FRIEND BONNIE AND I HAD JUST MOVED into a new *mansion* in the outskirts of Tokyo. Sounds impressive, I know, but unfortunately, a *mansion* in Japan boils down to a plain old apartment building. No moats, bodyguards, or other fancy thrills. Just a modern two-bedroom slab of concrete towering over a noisy, chaotic street.

I was in my fifth year of post-graduate studies in Japan, and I'd moved to Tokyo to complete my final research. It was nearly summer, and after lugging heavy boxes up and down stairs all day, I was more than ready to soak my sticky body in our new *o-furo*. I pushed the button next to the bath and twenty minutes later, a piercing *beep* shot through the flat, announcing that the bath water was ready to embrace my weary limbs.

I ripped off my filthy clothes, tossed them into the laundry basket, then scrubbed my whole body raw with a small rectangular towel (the Japanese don't use washcloths, but long towels, to make sure they cover every inch of grime

lodged in all private nooks and crannies). Next, I rinsed myself off—outside the bathtub—as Japanese custom obliges.

Once I was absolutely certain I was squeaky clean, I lowered a toe into the…hideously *cold* water. *Nani kore?* (What
the…?) I howled. Bath water in Japan tends to run uncomfortably hot, even scalding. I'd set the temperature to a
moderate 42 degrees Centigrade, but the tub was as chilly
as an Alaskan lake. That evening, I was no happy salmon,
that's for sure.

It was too late to call the concierge, so I lay out my futon
and pouted. I made a mental note to get our bath fixed the
next day. What an embarrassing experience *that* would turn
out to be!

"*Konnichi wa,*" the concierge greeted me, nervously bobbing his shiny head up and down. He seemed just as scared
to talk to me as most other Japanese men. Bonnie and I happened to be the only foreigners in the building, according to
our landlord, and from the way this guy was acting, I was
certain there hadn't been any before us.

"*Konnichi wa,*" I replied, then carefully explained our
o-furo problem.

"*Mondai nai*" he answered, no problem. "A maintenance
man will be by this afternoon," he promised me, in Japanese.
"Service in Japan sure is something!" I thought, relieved to
have the situation under control so quickly. I wandered back
to the apartment, to begin writing the first draft of my doctoral dissertation, due at the end of the month.

A few hours later, the doorbell chimed. A tall, beige-
uniformed man stood in my doorway, yet when he saw me,
he took a step back, then flushed like a steamy crab. He
bowed profusely as I ushered him into our *genkan*, or

entrance hall, where he removed his shoes, as is customary in Japan. Then I led him to our disobedient *o-furo*.

He whipped out a miniature digital camera and started flashing—mostly aiming at our bathtub and the pipes leading to its water heater. He said he'd need a few more minutes, to make sure he got everything.

As the bathroom was so tiny, the two of us could hardly fit inside, so I left him to take pictures and do whatever else he needed to repair the tub.

About ten minutes later, the flashing noises subsided, so I returned and asked him: "Is everything all right?"

"All's under control" he replied as he rushed out the door. "I'll be back later," he shot at me as he rammed his feet into his shoes and took off down the stairs.

I didn't expect the doorbell to chime again ten minutes later. But sure enough, it did and my tall friend came back with a short, skinny man in the same beige uniform. The skinny man bowed deeply to me as well, then they both removed their shoes and slid in their immaculate white socks towards the *o-furo*.

I left them alone and fifteen minutes later, I returned to find out how the repairs were coming. "Oh, no repairs yet. We need to check the measurements and take more pictures," the first man replied, pulling out his camera again. He snapped away at the walls, the ceiling, the laundry basket, etc.

"How many pictures do you *need* to fix a bathtub?" I asked him, suddenly annoyed.

"Almost done," he said, flashing two more times. Then they left.

Not more than five minutes later, I heard a knock on the door. "*Sumimasen*" (excuse me), someone whispered. I opened the door and three workers—the skinny guy and

two new ones—were lined up before me. They were carrying some heavy toolboxes.

"That was quick," I said to myself, relieved that the work
would finally get done. I led them into the bathroom once
again, then left them to do their repairs. I went back to the
kitchen, where I was painfully trying to concentrate on my
doctoral dissertation. I couldn't wait until the last of the
workers would finally be gone.

I heard some whispering, then someone laughed out
loud. The others followed. I couldn't make out the slightest
sounds of drilling, screwing, or hammering—just a steady
stream of manly giggles. Intrigued, I went over to see for
myself what the heck was wrong with my *o-furo*—it had to
be something wild, for them to let loose like that. "Is everything all right?" I queried.

"Yes, all right," said one. "We're almost done taking pictures," said another as he whipped another camera out of his
pants pocket. I stole a quick look at him, then at the other
two, who were squeezed into a corner of the bathroom. My
dirty laundry basket lay smack in between them. The lid was
off, and what did I see but Bonnie's and my used underwear—pink and bright yellow—gracefully sprawled over
the dingy heap.

I'd been planning to do our laundry that day, but with all
the interruptions, I hadn't had time. I gazed at our dirty
panties blatantly displayed before my guests, then scrutinized
those three shoeless *o-furo* workers. They appeared as if
they'd just stolen a heap of grandma's hot home-baked
cookies. Or a pile of *o-baachan*'s rice cakes, rather, since we
lived in Japan.

One worker was leaning to the side, trying to conceal the
lid of the laundry basket. That's when I remembered that I
had carefully covered the basket, because I didn't want any

workers seeing our dirty laundry. I understood at that moment that those five workers hadn't come to take pictures of our *o-furo*, they'd merely come to have a quick sniff of our used girly knickers.

Once I'd reached this conclusion, I pretty much threw the three out of my *mansion*. In Japan, of course it's not polite to be rude, but when you catch guys inhaling your private *pantsu*, or *rangelei* (just switch the "l" and the "r" and you get "lingerie"), I say you have a right to defend your territory. Especially if you're a female *gaijin* (foreigner), and you've got a serious deadline to make.

I *did* need my *o-furo* fixed though, so as I chucked them out, I tried to act like a respectable *gaijin*. I pretended I didn't know what was going on. The skinny one told me they'd be back the next day to fix the tub. They bowed like mad, then finally left me alone.

I slammed the door, then flew straight to the laundry basket. Sure enough, all the undies were on top. I counted four of mine and five of Bonnie's. A few lacy bras nestled underneath, as if searching for cover from those beige-clad *skebes* (dirty old farts). I tried to remember which panties I'd worn the past week, since I'd done the laundry last, and did some simple arithmetic in my head…

The conclusion was easy: in one week, I go through seven pairs of drawers, yet only four of mine could be found in the basket. That means, three pairs were missing…not including Bonnie's (who might be missing two, but I couldn't be 100 percent sure, for even though we were very close friends, I hadn't memorized her daily underwear habits).

In shock, I sat at the kitchen table and stared at my notes. After about an hour of struggling, I finally gave up on my dissertation. Thoughts of my dirty undies in someone else's pockets and printed on Fuji film overwhelmed me. I grabbed my backpack and left to go buy a few groceries. On my way down the stairs, I ran into two beige-uniformed men climbing up, with the same logo on their shirts as all the others.

The taller of the two stopped me, then had the nerve to ask me: "*Sumimasen*. Are you busy? Could we just see your bathroom, it won't take a minute."

I blew a fuse. "*Iie*" ("No." One *never* says "no" in Japan, it's not polite, but at that point, I could've ripped that man's neck off, which wouldn't have been very polite either. I chose the former solution.)

I certainly didn't have time to show two more workers my dirty drawers, and I *knew* they didn't need any more pictures of my tub. Plus, I was on my way out.

After my curt refusal, the man insisted, with: "What time are you returning? We can wait." As if all they had to do was sniff *gaijin* underwear all day long! No wonder they were incapable of repairing my *o-furo*. I told him off, as best I could, without worrying about the consequences. Bonnie and I could take showers for the next year—I couldn't care less at that point.

Amazingly enough, despite my foreign rudeness, the next day, two new men came to repair our tub. Just in case, I'd gotten up early to do all our laundry that morning and it was safely hanging outside to dry. I was sure I could read disappointment on their faces when they saw the empty laundry basket in our bathroom. So with no frilly, exotic, olfactory distractions, they kept their cameras at bay and swiftly repaired our *o-furo*.

Once the last pair of worker's shoes had left my *genkan*, I closed my front door, locked it, then sauntered straight to the bathroom. I gaily pushed the *o-furo* button and watched streams of boiling water rush into the tub. It was time to release some deep-seated physical and mental tensions caused by my painful twenty-four-hour cultural underwear crisis. I ripped my clothes off, tossed them into the laundry basket, scrubbed my body raw once again, then lowered a toe into the scalding water.

Laura Kline is a Belgian-American creative writer and translator living happily in Brussels with her partner and her fuzzy Calico cat. She came back from Japan in 2003 after obtaining her Master's and Ph.D. degrees, and spends her free time jotting down anecdotes from her crazy traveling experiences in Japan, Europe, and Mexico. She's currently working on learning her seventh language, and her dream is to write books and make films (comedies). She hopes that by sharing her odd, yet true international experiences, the world will become a playground for peace and love, instead of war.

⁕

Getting Grandma

It's important to know when to raise a stink.

THE NICELY DRESSED YOUNG MAN WHO HAD SHARED our compartment since Düsseldorf said goodbye in Munich, pressed a brown nugget the size of a hazelnut into the palm of my hand, and quickly got off the train.

"I think that guy just gave me a chunk of hash," I said to Yvette.

"You're kidding," she answered, looking at my hand. "No, you're not. That's amazing."

"What do you think I should do? Should I keep it?"

"Sure, why not? Just hide it somewhere. No one's gonna suspect us."

I don't know if it was some puritan ethic that stopped me from tossing a gift away, Yvette's confidence, or my evil twin named "curiosity," but I quickly stashed the little lump in my suitcase. And then forgot about it until the incident on the train in Yugoslavia when I learned what can happen when you never throw anything away.

It was Yugoslavia then, a communist country, not Slovenia,

Croatia, Macedonia, Serbia, Montenegro, Kosovo, Bosnia-Herzegovina. We were slicing through it on our way to Athens after enduring a cold late-October day in Salzburg. Snug in our sleeping car, Yvette on one bench, me on the other, we stretched our legs out, drank a morning cup of coffee, and lazily watched the foreign film unspooling outside the window. We were naïve Eurail travelers; it was our first trip to Europe. We didn't know we'd be sharing the compartment until the door opened at our last stop in Austria, and "Grandma" struggled in.

She wore a heavy dark blue sweater over a brown cotton dress spattered with small beige flowers. Her gray hair was pulled loosely into a bun. A jumble of bags hung from one arm; in the other, she held a baby.

Yvette quickly scooted to my side of the compartment. Grandma humphed down next to the window on the bench across from us. She snugged the baby into blankets and pillows on the seat beside her and smoothed her dress over her thick legs.

We smiled at her and said, "Hello." She answered with something we didn't understand. We pointed to the baby and smiled again. The baby made faces. Grandma gibbered more words we didn't understand and grinned. She was missing a front tooth.

Yvette decided that Grandma had been visiting her children in Austria and was now schlepping the grandchild to her village in Greece to give the parents a break. While Yvette was spinning her tale, Grandma began unwrapping bread, cheese, fruit, and jars filled with baby food. We were hungry and glad someone had brought food, especially home-made food. We nodded appreciatively, said, "Oh, that's nice, thank you," and offered her a soda. She took the soda and smiled her toothless grin. Then she fed the baby, ate her lunch, drank our soda, and tossed everything they didn't eat out the window.

In the field outside the train window, a woman in a long skirt and head scarf cutting hay with a scythe put down the curved blade and looked up from her work. A horse tethered to a wagon nearby swished its tail.

"That was really horrible," I said in a sweet voice to Grandma, knowing she didn't understand a word.

Yvette joined in, smiling at Grandma, "I hope you get a stomach ache and your other tooth falls out."

Grandma smiled back and began changing the baby's diaper. When she finished, she put the used diaper in a bag, and stuffed the bag under the bench.

"Did you see that?" Yvette hissed behind a hand held in front of her mouth, as if Grandma could understand. "She threw our lunch out the window and saved a disposable diaper."

"She must be going to toss it out later."

"No," said Yvette. "I saw another one inside. I don't think she knows they're disposable."

We shared a candy bar and read our books. When the baby started crying, we decided to look for a dining car. On the way, we had to elbow through a company of soldiers. Yvette used the "F" word to tell them to back the "F" off, and marched on, head high, her wild, curly black hair bouncing with every stomp. They may not have understood English, but they understood Yvette. I slipstreamed behind her.

The dining car was an oasis. Slightly shabby, but with a pedigree—the *Orient Express*'s poor cousin. On the walls, small bouquets carved with inlaid wood brightened the dingy mahogany panels. The lamps were antique, the table settings plain. It was the last car on the train; I could see farmland out the back window.

We didn't have Yugoslav money. We didn't have much money of any kind. There were no menus. A waiter came and tried to discourage us from ordering, or so it seemed. He didn't speak English. Because the train had stopped, Yvette decided he was telling us to wait until we started rolling again. Or maybe, she surmised, it was too late for lunch and the kitchen was closed until dinner. But, we were too hungry to wait.

We gathered all the coins we'd collected across Europe, put a pile of shillings, guilders, pfennigs, and marks on the table, and pled with the waiter by making sad faces and rubbing our bellies. He shrugged, took the coins and left. We waited, watching a group of men in blue work clothes near the train depot warm their hands over a fire in a metal garbage can. The buildings behind them were gray, concrete, faceless. A train whistle cried for attention.

Our waiter returned with steaming bowls of goulash, some crusty bread and two glasses of wine. We beamed at him. We would have eaten mush. As hungry as we were, though, we ate slowly, laughing, sharing stories, soup spoons clinking in the bowls. We had the cozy dining car to ourselves. No soldiers, no baby, no Grandma.

"This reminds me of something," Yvette said, pointing to a lamp. "Oh, I know. Our funky hotel in Amsterdam. What I remember most, though, was the look on your face when they said our room was on the fifth floor. I didn't think you'd ever be able to drag your suitcase up the stairs."

"Do you remember when we got lost that night walking back to the hotel?" I countered. "You tried to convince me the men staring at us in the cars driving by were commuters who had worked late. And then you looked up and saw the ladies in red corsets in the windows."

I swiped the last of the peppery goulash out of the bowl

with a piece of bread, sipped my wine, leaned back and
sighed. The train ride wouldn't be a disaster after all.

We decided to go back to our compartment, get our
books, and spend all our time in the dining car. I slid open
the door and stopped dead. Our dining car had been un-
hooked from the train and the train had moved a half a block
farther down the tracks.

"Omigod Yvette, the train's going to leave without us. We
have to go. Now!"

We leapt from the door of the dining car, ran alongside
the tracks past a clump of passengers who had gotten off the
train, and jumped on just as the whistle blew.

Shaken, pumped with adrenalin, we walked as quickly as
we could through the jostling cars, eager to reach our snug
compartment, Grandma or not. As we passed the first sleeping cars, we began to notice people moving suitcases around
and repacking. Yvette said they were preparing for bed.

We learned the real reason when we squeezed past a man
we thought was a ticket-taker to get to our compartment:
He was searching the luggage. And that's when I remembered my little hazelnut.

"Omigod Yvette," I whispered in her ear. "The hash."

Hands trembling, I opened our door and we collapsed
onto the bench. Grandma was just finishing another diaper
change. It looked like the baby had eaten too much fruit.

"What are you going to do?" Yvette asked me.

"I don't know," I whispered as the customs officer put
one highly polished shoe inside the door. The brass buttons
on his pristine uniform gleamed. He glowered.

"Passports," he said sternly. He slowly examined them,
checking our ashen faces against those of the happy young
women in the pictures. Then, he pulled Yvette's suitcase from

under the bench and opened it. Yvette and I sat stiffly, side by side, hands clasped in our laps, afraid to even blink. He shoved Yvette's suitcase aside with a grunt and opened the bag next to it.

It was Grandma's bag of dirty disposable diapers.

He couldn't get it closed. The smell ricocheted off the walls. It swam into our nostrils and crawled down our throats. The customs officer gagged. He gave us a sympathetic look. We smiled back sweetly. He stamped our passports as fast as he could, and left.

Yvette slammed open the window, stuck her head outside and gasped.

Grandma smiled and closed the bag.

I croaked from behind my hand, "Would you like another soda?"

Grandma got off the train at the first stop in Greece. We traveled on—to Athens and then to the islands. One day, on a beach in Mykonos, I gave my little hazelnut to a guy from Australia we had met a few hours earlier. He was leaving for Munich. We didn't have a pipe, anyway.

Barbara Robertson started traveling in the back seat of her father's Chevy and has been on the road as much as possible since. In addition to traveling for fun, her work as a journalist covering visual effects and animation has provided the ticket for journeys to many countries. When she's not packing or unpacking, she hangs out with her husband and three dogs in Mill Valley, California. She's won national and international awards for her articles, and writes regularly for The Hollywood Reporter, The Bark, Animation Magazine, Film & Video, Computer Graphics World, *and other publications.*

Index of Contributors

Acknowledgments

My biggest thanks goes to Susan Brady, Larry Habegger, James O'Reilly, and Sean O'Reilly who bust their butts to make sure these women's travel humor books go out in top form. I love them like family, and their friendship is more important to me than any amount of book sales. Thanks also to our production assistant, Christy Harrington, and our interns, Emily Dunn and Lydia Harari, who generously gave their time and effort to this book. And the book would not get its good looks without the creative brainstorming from Peter Ginelli, the participation of Jaime McFadden, and the devoted hard work of Stefan Gutermuth.

We owe all belly laughs about the title to Jeremy Balka. Jer, I thoroughly appreciate you working out the statistical probabilities of what words would generate the most amount of guffaws…we love it, no matter what the conservatives say!

Continued thanks to Sean Keener, Chris Heidrich, and the BootsnAll staff who keep my websites running and my online following growing by leaps and bounds. It's deeply meaningful to have you believing in me and helping to make my dreams come true.

Heartfelt appreciation to my writing sisters Lauren Cuthbert, Lynn Ferrin, Danielle Machotka, Linda Watanabe McFerrin, Christi Phillips, and Alison Wright. Thank you so much for guiding me and remaining my biggest fans.

And as always, I couldn't go anywhere or do anything crazy without the love, strength, and friendship of my family and second families. They give me their guestrooms, do my work for me, act as airport shuttle drivers and storage units, send happy pictures of their kids, donate emergency funds, inspire me to achieve more—

and always give me unconditional invitations to come home despite large holes in my communication efforts. I love you all right back and I went alphabetical with this because you're all A-List in my book:

Kelly Amabile, Jessica Balesteri and Scott Hennis, Jim Benning, the Bradys, Dan Buczaczer and Jennifer Porcinito, Mike and Pat Buczaczer, John Caldwell, Sally Caton, Jennifer Colvin and Bob Read, Nathaniel Eaton, Merle Hammond and Max Abbott, the Heidrichs, Scott Gimple, Jacob Glezer and Judy Persky and family, Phil Gordon, Heather and Mark Grennan and family, the Lyons family, Rolf Potts, Leigh and Seth Presant and family, Lisa and Mike Ramsey, Bridget Burke Ravissa and family, Viv and Josh Spoerri and family, Oscar Villalon and Mary Ladd, the Walshs, Tara Weaver, and Dana and Brian Welsh and my sweet god daughters Berklee and Reilly.

And last but not least, my family. All the Leos, both West Coast and East Coast. Marylin Livingston and all the Livingstons (plus those who've changed their names). Extra special hugs to my dad, Garry L. Leo, who lets me call him at any hour of the night. Thank you so much for believing in me…(and not reading my risqué stories!)

About the Editor

Jennifer L. Leo is a magnet for misadventure and always ready to gamble on having a good time. She is the editor of the best-selling Travelers' Tales women's humor series, including the award-winning *Sand in My Bra* and *Whose Panties Are These?* You can find Jen's writing in books and magazines such as *A Woman's Passion for Travel, Hyenas Laughed at Me and Now I Know Why, Lonely Planet The Best of Las Vegas, TIME, Playboy, Audrey, Student Traveler*, and *Women Poker Player*, among others. She is also known as a professional blogger. WrittenRoad.com, her online resource for travel writers, was named one of *Writer's Digest's* 101 Best Websites for Writers. She lives in Las Vegas where she writes for VivaLasVegasBlog.com between adventures in the poker world. Check in with JenLeo.com to see what she's up to next.

TRAVELERS' TALES
THE POWER OF A GOOD STORY

New Releases

THE BEST TRAVEL WRITING 2005 $16.95
True Stories from Around the World
Edited by James O'Reilly, Larry Habegger & Sean O'Reilly
The second in a new annual series presenting fresh, lively storytelling
and compelling narrative to make the reader laugh, weep, and buy a
plane ticket.

IT'S A DOG'S WORLD $14.95
True Stories of Travel with Man's Best Friend
Edited by Christine Hunsicker
Introduction by Maria Goodavage
Hilarious and heart warming stories of traveling with canine companions.

A SENSE OF PLACE $18.95
**Great Travel Writers Talk About Their Craft, Lives,
and Inspiration**
By Michael Shapiro
A stunning collection of interviews with the world's leading travel writers,
including: Isabel Allende, Bill Bryson, Tim Cahill, Arthur Frommer, Pico Iyer,
Peter Matthiessen, Frances Mayes, Jan Morris, Redmond O'Hanlon, Jonathan
Raban, Paul Theroux, Simon Winchester, and many more.

WHOSE PANTIES ARE THESE? $14.95
More Misadventures from Funny Women on the Road
Edited by Jennifer L. Leo
Following on the high heels of the award-winning bestseller *Sand in My
Bra and other Misadventures* comes another collection of hilarious travel
stories by women.

SAFETY AND SECURITY FOR WOMEN WHO TRAVEL (SECOND EDITION) $14.95
By Sheila Swan & Peter Laufer
"A cache of valuable advice."   —*The Christian Science Monitor*

A WOMAN'S PASSION FOR TRAVEL $17.95
True Stories of World Wanderlust
Edited by Marybeth Bond & Pamela Michael
"A diverse and gripping series of stories!"   —Arlene Blum, author of
Annapurna: A Woman's Place

THE GIFT OF TRAVEL $14.95
Inspiring Stories from Around the World
Edited by Larry Habegger, James O'Reilly & Sean O'Reilly
"Like gourmet chefs in a French market, the editors of Travelers' Tales pick, sift,
and prod their way through the weighty shelves of contemporary travel writing,
creaming off the very best."   —William Dalrymple, author of *City of Djinns*

Women's Travel

A WOMAN'S EUROPE $17.95
True Stories
Edited by Marybeth Bond
An exhilarating collection of inspirational, adventurous, and entertaining stories by women exploring the romantic continent of Europe. From the bestselling author Marybeth Bond.

WOMEN IN THE WILD $17.95
True Stories of Adventure and Connection
Edited by Lucy McCauley
"A spiritual, moving, and totally female book to take you around the world and back."
—*Mademoiselle*

A MOTHER'S WORLD $14.95
Journeys of the Heart
Edited by Marybeth Bond & Pamela Michael
"These stories remind us that motherhood is one of the great unifying forces in the world."
—*San Francisco Examiner*

A WOMAN'S PATH $16.95
Women's Best Spiritual Travel Writing
Edited by Lucy McCauley, Amy G. Carlson & Jennifer Leo
"A sensitive exploration of women's lives that have been unexpectedly and spiritually touched by travel experiences.... Highly recommended."
—*Library Journal*

A WOMAN'S WORLD $18.95
True Stories of World Travel
Edited by Marybeth Bond
Introduction by Dervla Murphy

—— ★★★ ——

Lowell Thomas Award
—Best Travel Book

A WOMAN'S PASSION FOR TRAVEL $17.95
True Stories of World Wanderlust
Edited by Marybeth Bond & Pamela Michael
"A diverse and gripping series of stories!"
—Arlene Blum, author of
Annapurna: A Woman's Place

Food

ADVENTURES IN WINE $17.95
True Stories of Vineyards and Vintages around the World
Edited by Thom Elkjer
Humanity, community, and brotherhood compose the marvelous virtues of the wine world. This collection toasts the warmth and wonders of this large extended family in stories by travelers who are wine novices and experts alike.

HER FORK IN THE ROAD $16.95
Women Celebrate Food and Travel
Edited by Lisa Bach
A savory sampling of stories by the best writers in and out of the food and travel fields.

FOOD $18.95
A Taste of the Road
Edited by Richard Sterling
Introduction by Margo True

—— ★★★ ——

Silver Medal Winner of the
Lowell Thomas Award
—Best Travel Book

THE ADVENTURE OF FOOD $17.95
True Stories of Eating Everything
Edited by Richard Sterling
"Bound to whet appetites for more than food."
—*Publishers Weekly*

HOW TO EAT AROUND THE WORLD $12.95
Tips and Wisdom
By Richard Sterling
Combines practical advice on foodstuffs, habits, and etiquette, with hilarious accounts of others' eating adventures.

Travel Humor

SAND IN MY BRA AND OTHER MISADVENTURES $14.95
Funny Women Write from the Road
Edited by Jennifer L. Leo
"A collection of ridiculous and sublime travel experiences."
— *San Francisco Chronicle*

LAST TROUT IN VENICE $14.95
The Far-Flung Escapades of an Accidental Adventurer
By Doug Lansky
"Traveling with Doug Lansky might result in a considerably shortened life expectancy...but what a way to go."
— Tony Wheeler, Lonely Planet Publications

THERE'S NO TOILET PAPER ON THE ROAD LESS TRAVELED $12.95
The Best of Travel Humor and Misadventure
Edited by Doug Lansky —— ✶ * ✶ ——

—— ✶ * ✶ —— *ForeWord Gold Medal Winner — Humor Book of the Year*
Humor Book of the Year Independent Publisher's Book Award

HYENAS LAUGHED AT ME AND NOW I KNOW WHY $14.95
The Best of Travel Humor and Misadventure
Edited by Sean O'Reilly, Larry Habegger & James O'Reilly
Hilarious, outrageous and reluctant voyagers indulge us with the best misadventures around the world.

NOT SO FUNNY WHEN IT HAPPENED $12.95
The Best of Travel Humor and Misadventure
Edited by Tim Cahill
Laugh with Bill Bryson, Dave Barry, Anne Lamott, Adair Lara, and many more.

WHOSE PANTIES ARE THESE? $14.95
More Misadventures from Funny Women on the Road
Edited by Jennifer L. Leo
Following on the high heels of the award-winning bestseller *Sand in My Bra and other Misadventures* comes another collection of hilarious travel stories by women.

Travelers' Tales Classics

COAST TO COAST $16.95
A Journey Across 1950s America
By Jan Morris
After reporting on the first Everest ascent in 1953, Morris spent a year journeying across the United States. In brilliant prose, Morris records with exuberance and curiosity a time of innocence in the U.S.

THE ROYAL ROAD TO ROMANCE $14.95
By Richard Halliburton
"Laughing at hardships, dreaming of beauty, ardent for adventure, Halliburton has managed to sing into the pages of this glorious book his own exultant spirit of youth and freedom."
— *Chicago Post*

TRADER HORN $16.95
A Young Man's Astounding Adventures in 19th Century Equatorial Africa
By Alfred Aloysius Horn
Here is the stuff of legends—thrills and danger, wild beasts, serpents, and savages. An unforgettable and vivid portrait of a vanished Africa.

UNBEATEN TRACKS IN JAPAN $14.95
By Isabella L. Bird
Isabella Bird was one of the most adventurous women travelers of the 19th century with journeys to Tibet, Canada, Korea, Turkey, Hawaii, and Japan. A fascinating read.

THE RIVERS RAN EAST $16.95
By Leonard Clark
Clark is the original Indiana Jones, telling the breathtaking story of his search for the legendary El Dorado gold in the Amazon.

Spiritual Travel

THE SPIRITUAL GIFTS OF TRAVEL $16.95
The Best of Travelers' Tales
Edited by James O'Reilly & Sean O'Reilly
Favorite stories of transformation on the road that show the myriad ways travel indelibly alters our inner landscapes.

PILGRIMAGE $16.95
Adventures of the Spirit
Edited by Sean O'Reilly & James O'Reilly
Introduction by Phil Cousineau

ForeWord Silver Medal Winner
—Travel Book of the Year

THE ROAD WITHIN $18.95
True Stories of Transformation and the Soul
Edited by Sean O'Reilly, James O'Reilly & Tim O'Reilly

Independent Publisher's Book Award
—Best Travel Book

THE WAY OF THE WANDERER $14.95
Discover Your True Self Through Travel
By David Yeadon
Experience transformation through travel with this delightful, illustrated collection by award-winning author David Yeadon.

A WOMAN'S PATH $16.95
Women's Best Spiritual Travel Writing
Edited by Lucy McCauley, Amy G. Carlson & Jennifer Leo
"A sensitive exploration of women's lives that have been unexpectedly and spiritually touched by travel experiences.... Highly recommended."
—*Library Journal*

THE ULTIMATE JOURNEY $17.95
Inspiring Stories of Living and Dying
James O'Reilly, Sean O'Reilly & Richard Sterling
"A glorious collection of writings about the ultimate adventure. A book to keep by one's bedside—and close to one's heart."
—Philip Zaleski, editor,
The Best Spiritual Writing series

Special Interest

THE BEST TRAVELERS' TALES 2004 $16.95
True Stories from Around the World
Edited by James O'Reilly, Larry Habegger & Sean O'Reilly
"This book will grace my bedside for years to come."
—Simon Winchester, from the Introduction

TESTOSTERONE PLANET $17.95
True Stories from a Man's World
Edited by Sean O'Reilly, Larry Habegger & James O'Reilly
Thrills and laughter with some of today's best writers, including Sebastian Junger, Tim Cahill, Bill Bryson, and Jon Krakauer.

THE GIFT OF TRAVEL $14.95
Inspiring Stories from Around the World
Edited by Larry Habegger, James O'Reilly & Sean O'Reilly
"Like gourmet chefs in a French market, the editors of Travelers' Tales pick, sift, and prod their way through the weighty shelves of contemporary travel writing, creaming off the very best."
—William Dalrymple, author of *City of Djinns*

DANGER! $17.95
True Stories of Trouble and Survival
Edited by James O'Reilly, Larry Habegger & Sean O'Reilly
"Exciting...for those who enjoy living on the edge or prefer to read the survival stories of others, this is a good pick."
—*Library Journal*

365 TRAVEL $14.95
A Daily Book of Journeys, Meditations, and Adventures
Edited by Lisa Bach
An illuminating collection of travel wisdom and adventures that reminds us all of the lessons we learn while on the road.

THE GIFT OF RIVERS $14.95
True Stories of Life on the Water
Edited by Pamela Michael
Introduction by Robert Hass
"...a soulful compendium of wonderful stories that illuminate, educate, inspire, and delight."
    —David Brower,
Chairman of Earth Island Institute

FAMILY TRAVEL $17.95
The Farther You Go, the Closer You Get
Edited by Laura Manske
"This is family travel at its finest."
    —*Working Mother*

LOVE & ROMANCE $17.95
True Stories of Passion on the Road
Edited by Judith Babcock Wylie
"A wonderful book to read by a crackling fire."
    —*Romantic Traveling*

THE GIFT OF BIRDS $17.95
True Encounters with Avian Spirits
Edited by Larry Habegger & Amy G. Carlson
"These are all wonderful, entertaining stories offering a *bird's-eye view!* of our avian friends."
    —*Booklist*

IT'S A DOG'S WORLD $14.95
True Stories of Travel with Man's Best Friend
Edited by Christine Hunsicker
Introduction by Maria Goodavage
Hilarious and heart warming stories of traveling with canine companions.

Travel Advice

THE PENNY PINCHER'S PASSPORT TO LUXURY TRAVEL $14.95 (2ND EDITION)
The Art of Cultivating Preferred Customer Status
By Joel L. Widzer
Completely updated and revised, this 2nd edition of the popular guide to traveling like the rich and famous without being either describes, both philosophically and in practical terms, how to obtain luxurious travel benefits by building relationships with airlines and other travel companies.

SAFETY AND SECURITY FOR WOMEN WHO TRAVEL (2ND EDITION) $14.95
By Sheila Swan & Peter Laufer
"A cache of valuable advice."
    —*The Christian Science Monitor*

THE FEARLESS SHOPPER $14.95
How to Get the Best Deals on the Planet
By Kathy Borrus
"Anyone who reads *The Fearless Shopper* will come away a smarter, more responsible shopper and a more curious, culturally attuned traveler."
    —Jo Mancuso, *The Shopologist*

SHITTING PRETTY $12.95
How to Stay Clean and Healthy While Traveling
By Dr. Jane Wilson-Howarth
A light-hearted book about a serious subject for millions of travelers—staying healthy on the road—written by international health expert, Dr. Jane Wilson-Howarth.

GUTSY WOMEN (2ND EDITION) $12.95
More Travel Tips and Wisdom for the Road
By Marybeth Bond
Packed with funny, instructive, and inspiring advice for women heading out to see the world.

GUTSY MAMAS $7.95
Travel Tips and Wisdom for Mothers on the Road
By Marybeth Bond
A delightful guide for mothers traveling with their children—or without them!

Destination Titles

ALASKA   **$18.95**
Edited by Bill Sherwonit, Andromeda Romano-Lax, & Ellen Bielawski

AMERICA   **$19.95**
Edited by Fred Setterberg

AMERICAN SOUTHWEST   **$17.95**
Edited by Sean O'Reilly & James O'Reilly

AUSTRALIA   **$18.95**
Edited by Larry Habegger

BRAZIL   **$18.95**
Edited by Annette Haddad & Scott Doggett
Introduction by Alex Shoumatoff

CENTRAL AMERICA   **$17.95**
Edited by Larry Habegger & Natanya Pearlman

CHINA   **$18.95**
Edited by Sean O'Reilly, James O'Reilly & Larry Habegger

CUBA   **$18.95**
Edited by Tom Miller

FRANCE   **$18.95**
Edited by James O'Reilly, Larry Habegger & Sean O'Reilly

GRAND CANYON   **$17.95**
Edited by Sean O'Reilly, James O'Reilly & Larry Habegger

GREECE   **$18.95**
Edited by Larry Habegger, Sean O'Reilly & Brian Alexander

HAWAI'I   **$17.95**
Edited by Rick & Marcie Carroll

HONG KONG   **$17.95**
Edited by James O'Reilly, Larry Habegger & Sean O'Reilly

INDIA   **$19.95**
Edited by James O'Reilly & Larry Habegger

IRELAND   **$18.95**
Edited by James O'Reilly, Larry Habegger & Sean O'Reilly

Footsteps Series

THE FIRE NEVER DIES $14.95
One Man's Raucous Romp Down the Road of Food,
Passion, and Adventure
By Richard Sterling
"Sterling's writing is like spitfire, foursquare and jazzy with
crackle...."   *—Kirkus Reviews*

ONE YEAR OFF $14.95
Leaving It All Behind for a Round-the-World Journey
with Our Children
By David Elliot Cohen
A once-in-a-lifetime adventure generously shared, from the
author/editor of *America 24/7* and *A Day in the Life of Africa*

THE WAY OF THE WANDERER $14.95
Discover Your True Self Through Travel
By David Yeadon
Experience transformation through travel with this delightful,
illustrated collection by award-winning author David Yeadon.

TAKE ME WITH YOU $24.00
A Round-the-World Journey to Invite a Stranger Home
By Brad Newsham
"Newsham is an ideal guide. His journey, at heart, is into
humanity."   —Pico Iyer, author of *The Global Soul*

KITE STRINGS OF THE SOUTHERN CROSS $14.95
A Woman's Travel Odyssey
By Laurie Gough   *ForeWord Silver Medal Winner*
Short-listed for the prestigious Thomas Cook Award, this is an   *— Travel Book of the Year*
exquisite rendering of a young woman's search for meaning.

                              ★ ★ ★

THE SWORD OF HEAVEN $24.00
A Five Continent Odyssey to Save the World
By Mikkel Aaland
"Few books capture the soul of the road like The *Sword of
Heaven,* a sharp-edged, beautifully rendered memoir that will
inspire anyone."
       —Phil Cousineau, author of *The Art of Pilgrimage*

STORM $24.00
A Motorcycle Journey of Love, Endurance,   *ForeWord Gold Medal Winner*
and Transformation   *— Travel Book of the Year*
By Allen Noren
"Beautiful, tumultuous, deeply engaging and very satisfying.   ★ ★ ★
Anyone who looks for truth in travel will find it here."
       —Ted Simon, author of *Jupiter's Travels*